MODERN
FRENCH
COOKING

MODERN FRENCH COOKING

Rae Spurlock

Nelson
Hall
nh
Chicago

Library of Congress Cataloging in Publication Data

Spurlock, Rae, 1941–
Modern French cooking.

Includes index.
1. Cookery, French. I. Title.
TX719.S68   641.5′944   79-23751
ISBN 0-88229-480-6

Manufactured in the United States of America

10   9   8   7   6   5   4   3   2   1

for Will

CONTENTS

Introduction

The gift of French food is a legacy we continue to enjoy. As a means of fulfilling both a need and a pleasure in our lives, the French approach to cooking is as vital today as in the past. Food prepared the French way, with attention to detail, preparation, and serving, does more than satisfy hunger; it appeals to an aesthetic sense as well. Meals served this way add a higher dimension to daily living. But today, the selection and preparation of food must also meet other criteria. The modern way of cooking in the old French manner reflects our increased knowledge of nutrition, a fluctuating economy, changes in family size, and, most important, changes in our living patterns.

Modern French cooking is leaner and lighter because we live, for the most part, more sedentary lives and simply do not require a feast every day. We have recently learned that the flavors of wines, stocks, and herbs are sufficiently rich that sauces made from them do not require the additional enrichment of butter. To slim modern cooking even more, unneeded fat from browning meat is always discarded, and stocks and sauces are skimmed of as much fat as possible.

Similarly, recipes today need not be measured to feed an army because most people cook only for themselves and one to three others. Today we worry more about how to divide and subtract the remainders of what we cook than how to prepare it in the first place. That brings us to the point which sets this cookbook apart from others.

All cookbooks discuss the initial preparation of foods. This one is equally concerned with uses for foods that have already been cooked once, especially meats. In presenting this system of cooking, all the important initial cooking methods have been utilized—poaching, braising, roasting, sautéing, deep-frying, and broiling—and every effort has been made to follow up with suggestions for serving the remaining food. In this regard, some new techniques have been devised which permit previously roasted meat to be used in stews. Heretofore, this was thought to be impossible, but if these recipes are followed exactly the meat will not lose its quality or flavor. This has obvious economic advantages since, besides permitting total use of the food purchased, it also provides an incentive to plan meals around the larger cuts of meat which are less expensive than steaks and chops.

Other extensions of meat cookery are found in Chapters 5 and 7. Sauces and soups are developed from the concentrated pan sauces of roasted or braised meats. These supplemental methods will be particularly useful to those who cook for smaller families. The methods in this book may easily be adapted to suit the needs of singles who live alone and often cook only for themselves. A little planning in advance will relieve a steady diet of frozen potpies. All the recipes in this book serve about four people but they may be halved or doubled as necessary. It is always best, however, to cook to scale since previously cooked food can be reheated only once without risking nutritional loss.

There is a misconception that French cooking is costly because it requires excellent ingredients: butter and high-quality oils, the freshest vegetables and fish, wines and meat of the best grade. Actually, the French have contrived the most ingenious devices for the conscientious use of foods. Classic cooking is a system in which everything has a purpose and the parts are interrelated. Bones are not discarded; they are a necessary part of stockmaking. Even partial servings of vegetables, cooked meats, and fish may be beautifully arranged as hors d'oeuvre, or added to soups and salads. Soufflés, crêpes, and croquettes offer glamorous solutions to leftovers. Stocks from simmered meats are used to make soup, or to create sauces for other meats and vegetables. With rising costs of food and potential future shortages, this approach to cooking takes on a new validity.

Another reason for reviving an old manner of cooking is the beneficial effect it has on health. Cooking with fresh, natural foods unaltered by preservatives and artificial flavorings is the original "health food" approach to cooking. Even those who refrain from consuming alcohol may cook with wine because the alcohol it contains is always burned out over high heat before other food is cooked in it.

Cooking according to this scheme does not take more time than standard American methods, but it may, at first, require more thought given to planning. For instance, stockmaking is no effort whatsoever. A stock can simmer unattended on a back burner, but one must think ahead to do it. Most dishes are actually easier to prepare than the common, American "casserole." Many recipes, in whole or in part, may be prepared in advance. In our household we cook no other way. My husband and I frequently share the necessities (and pleasures) of cooking as we both have demanding, time-consuming careers. These techniques and methods are not beyond the capabilities of our children, who also have cooking responsibilities. A friend once said, "If you can make a white sauce, you can make anything!'' Our daughter has proved the truth of this statement by creating very elegant dishes from a knowledge of that simple technique. With forethought, the methods in this book may be accomplished by the least sophisticated cook and accommodated by the busiest lifestyle.

The purpose of this book is to coordinate many such ideas into a convenient form. Its structure is a diverse collection of recipes woven into a workable plan for cooking. You will be able to take any meat, fish, or vegetable, cooked or uncooked, and do something exciting with it. Most importantly, it will enable you to cook in the best continental manner, every day.

Note on Symbols. In the text, * indicates a recipe that may be found by consulting the Index; † denotes a word defined in the Glossary.

Note of Appreciation.

My sincerest thanks and gratitude to the editors at Nelson-Hall for their sensitive and exceedingly professional editing of this text, to Pam Teisler for her special labors with the tedious complexities of the format, to Dick Epler for sustained support throughout the process of production, and to William Steubing for considering the manuscript in the first place! And to the other staff at Nelson-Hall in their efforts to see this project to completion I am most appreciative.

Rae Spurlock

The Supply Shelf

There is nothing exotic about the foods used to create the dishes in this book. The full, rich stocks that are the foundation of soups, sauces, and stews derive much of their flavor from:

    carrots,
    onions, and
    bones,

and from an herb "bouquet" made by adding:

    celery,
    parsley,
    bay leaf, and just a pinch of
    thyme.

The last two are commonly available in the spice section of any supermarket. Sometimes, instead of onion, there is a requirement for the stronger overtones of

    garlic.

Garlic may be prepared for cooking by separating the clove from the head. Place the clove on a cutting board beneath the handle of a heavy knife. Give a sharp blow with the knife handle, crushing the clove of garlic underneath. Now the garlic may be easily peeled and chopped, if necessary. A more refined flavor for fillings or pan deglazing† sauces is achieved by using

    green onions or, if available in the supermarket produce section,
    shallots.

Shallots look like little onions and have a mild flavor "between" garlic and onion. Brown (gravy) sauces obtain greater richness with the addition of a small amount of

    tomato paste,

while the flavor of white (cream) sauces is heightened with drops of
    fresh lemon juice.

Lemon is usually required for fish and certain marinades and may, in some cases, be substituted for wine in braising. Other herbs and spices

needed from time to time are:
> basil, oregano, marjoram,
> rosemary and tarragon,
> saffron, dill, and fennel,
> cinnamon and ginger,
> nutmeg, allspice, and cloves.

The browning of most meat is done in a good quality, flavorless oil such as corn oil, or other polyunsaturated vegetable oil.

This oil may also be used in vinaigrette sauce.* To maintain freshness after opening, oil should be stored in the refrigerator. Vinaigrette sauce receives an added flavor boost from
> Dijon (French-style) mustard,

found with condiments or "gourmet" foods in most supermarkets. There really is no substitute for
> butter,

but since it is generally used sparingly, its use need not be a threat to waistlines. In modern cooking, butter enrichments are usually omitted, but occasionally sauces are given distinction with the addition of spoonfuls of
> heavy cream.

This may be thinned with milk when a lighter cream is called for. For use in soups, salads, sauces, toppings, and on the dessert tray, always have a supply of a good
> Swiss cheese.

In one form or another,
> beef and chicken stocks

should be available at all times. Stocks, marinades, and sauces derive character from dry table wines (see chapter 3). The most versatile choices for white and red wines are
> Chablis and Claret.

Never cook with a wine that is not good enough to drink. If, however, a wine should turn during storage it may be used as
> wine vinegar.

Less often you will need
> Cognac and Madeira (wine)

but it is a good idea to keep them on hand. They store very well even after opening.

Tomatoes and mushrooms are often used but should be purchased fresh when needed. A number of recipes require tomatoes "peeled, seeded, juiced, and chopped." There is an easy method for preparing them:

Drop the tomatoes into boiling water to cover for about 10 seconds. Drain and plunge them into cold water. The skins will slip off easily when carefully pierced with a knife. Cut in half and gently remove seeds and excess juice with forefinger.

Tomatoes are seeded for appearance' sake only. From the standpoint of nutrition in everyday cooking it is better to retain the seeds and juice. Do not peel tomatoes to be used in salads. However, they should be peeled when used in stews, otherwise the skins will detach and float unattractively in the stock.

With these basic supplies the possibilities for creative invention are unlimited. Most of the finest achievements of culinary history may be reproduced from this humble list.

Equipment

One needn't own a vast inventory of cooking utensils in order to perform any of the operations in this text. Improvisation and imagination are the most important assets to acquire. In addition to the ordinary. equipment found in any kitchen only a few items should be noted.

A blender is a valuable aid but since it cannot process uncooked meats, a grinder is an absolute necessity. Use good quality wooden spoons that will not split. If you do not already have one, purchase a medium-sized wire whip at the supermarket.

Invest in heavy, enameled, cast-iron cookware. A complete set is not required because four strategic pieces will perform nearly all the necessary functions (see illustration). Use a heavy, steep-sided, *non*-enameled pan or Dutch oven for deep fat frying.

Adaptations for Vegetable Cookery

A potato ricer is required for the new technique with puréed potatoes and you will need racks for steaming vegetables. These may be easily fabricated and will enable you to convert the versatile heavy casseroles into vegetable steamers.

The large shallow casserole (A) is used for most vegetables cooked by steaming methods. A "shelf" is inserted onto the pan bottom to hold the vegetables over the cooking water. A 12-inch (30 cm) round splatter screen of meshed aluminum may be used effectively for this purpose.

To make a rack for the oval roaster (B) for steaming artichokes, trim the sides of a 5x8x2-inch (12.5x20x5 cm) disposable aluminum pan so that the sides measure 1-inch (2.5 cm). Then, to make steam holes, set the pan, trimmed edge up, on a cake rack. Plunge a pick or shish kebab skewer through the bottom of the pan, ventilating it with as many holes as possible.

5

A. A large, shallow casserole with a tight-fitting, heavy lid braises chops and beef rolls. The bottom is also used as a skillet for sautéing chicken. Use it without the lid for open pan roasting in the oven.

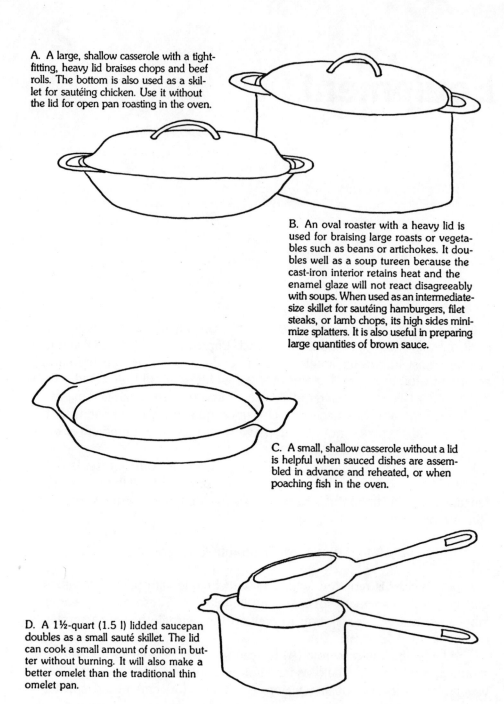

B. An oval roaster with a heavy lid is used for braising large roasts or vegetables such as beans or artichokes. It doubles well as a soup tureen because the cast-iron interior retains heat and the enamel glaze will not react disagreeably with soups. When used as an intermediate-size skillet for sautéing hamburgers, filet steaks, or lamb chops, its high sides minimize splatters. It is also useful in preparing large quantities of brown sauce.

C. A small, shallow casserole without a lid is helpful when sauced dishes are assembled in advance and reheated, or when poaching fish in the oven.

D. A 1½-quart (1.5 l) lidded saucepan doubles as a small sauté skillet. The lid can cook a small amount of onion in butter without burning. It will also make a better omelet than the traditional thin omelet pan.

Enameled, Cast-Iron Cookware

Use of a Meat Thermometer in the Roasting Method

In traditional cooking, the "doneness" of roasted meat was determined by *touch* and *smell*. The ability to judge when a particular meat is à point comes with experience. That "point" of doneness varies with the kind of meat. Beef and lamb are said to be à point when medium-rare, veal and pork, when well done. Beef and lamb cease to be soft and become resistant to the touch when they are "to the point." When meat is cooked to the perfect degree, it will suddenly flood the kitchen with its full aroma. These are sensory signs that have largely been lost to us. But, restoring an awareness of them is part of the process of becoming a sensitive and responsive cook.

For various reasons, a meat thermometer can aid in judging doneness. If a roast is smaller than the size described in a recipe, it may be ready sooner than indicated. Ovens vary drastically when they are inaccurately calibrated or if they are smaller than standard. Such factors can affect cooking times. In these cases, a thermometer provides a helpful double-check.

A thermometer must be inserted properly to get a true reading of internal temperature. The end of the thermometer must reach, as nearly as possible, the center of the thickest part of the roast. In placing it, however, the tip must not touch a bone, thick cartilage, or membranes.

In the final analysis, the right degree of doneness is achieved by balancing these factors (the objective thermometer and the subjective response of the senses) with personal taste. Even though traditional standards recommend beef be cooked to medium-rare, many people do not eat beef that is not roasted to "well-done." The following chart correlates the degree of doneness for various types of meat with the internal temperature readings on a meat thermometer.

Internal Temperature of Roasted Meats

BEEF	Fahrenheit	Celsius
rare	136°	52°
medium-rare	140°	54°
medium	155°	62°
well-done	170°	69°
LAMB		
medium-rare	145°	57°
well-done	160°	64°
PORK	180°	74°
VEAL	175°	72°
CHICKEN	180°	74°

Fruit of the Vine

3

The dominant theme of this book is careful attention to planning. One of the more pleasurable benefits of economizing is the chance to invest in good wines for cooking and serving. Thus, this chapter provides the raison d'être of modern French cooking. When one invests time in careful planning, sensible marketing, and far-sighted preparation, one is afforded the joy (and I would say, the necessity) of a lovely wine with dinner.

The longstanding European tradition of serving good wine with good food is customary for many people. Moreover, given the pace of contemporary life, it is more important than ever that dinner be a time to relax fully and set aside the concerns of the day. Together, food and wine generate a sense of weil-being and bring the day to a satisfying conclusion. Wine complements every food and every occasion. It can appropriately mark a celebration or be tucked into a picnic basket. Wine is for every day.

An interest in the preparation of good food seems to lead inevitably to an interest in wine. Together they become daily pleasures. Even given a lifetime, it would be impossible to learn everything there is to know about wine, impossible to try each variation. But if the escalating wine sales of recent years are any indication, American interest in exploring the world's wines is increasing. Like wine-lovers everywhere, Americans are developing a curiosity about the nuance and subtlety of different bottles, varieties, and vintages.

Wine and Health

There are important dietary reasons for including a dry table wine with dinner. Most wines have a relatively low alcohol content (twelve percent, or twenty-four proof). Unlike other spirits, wine usually is not drunk for its alcoholic effect. Even serious tasters, exploring many wines at a time, do not swallow the samples. The wine drinker is interested in a wine's fragrance, or its bouquet, the essence of its flavor, the clarity, richness, or delicacy of its color, and the texture of its body.

9

As with all things, it is quality, not quantity, that matters. One's interest and appreciation cultivates a discerning taste that, if anything, serves to restrain overindulgence. A true gourmet (of food) and connoisseur (of wine) is more concerned with refining an everyday aspect of life than with mere consumption.

Table wine is a light and slimming drink. A four-ounce glass has only about sixty-four calories. A natural beverage, to which no additional sugar is added, it contains vitamin B, iron, and many other minerals. In moderate quantities wine effectively promotes digestion and acts as a safe aid to relaxation. A meal served with wine does not set heavily or uncomfortably in the stomach, and it is frequently recommended by doctors for these benefits.

Background Basics: Grape Growing and Processing

Knowledgeable wine selection rests mainly on experience. The difficulty most people encounter comes initially: they simply do not know where to begin. Faced with a sea of American and imported wine labels, the probability of error increases. This chapter is a basic introduction to wine, and it includes a wine selection chart and a label reading guide. Recipes to follow in this book refer to a range of appropriate choices listed on the wine chart. From that range the reader may make the specific wine selection for a dish.

Actually, with a few basic principles in mind, learning to select the correct wine is no more difficult than deciding on an appropriate sauce for a meat. In both, there are few serious "mistakes" one can make and just a little background knowledge minimizes the likelihood of errors.

Before discussing wine types, we will begin by looking at the factors that influence grape growing and processing. Such factors bear ultimately on the quality of the bottle on the dealer's shelf. Years of study may be devoted to understanding these details and the specific differences they effect. For our purposes, it is enough just to recognize some features relevant to the process.

The principal factors which shape the wine are the regional climate and the nature of the soil in which the grapes are grown. German wines demonstrate these points well: their character and quality vary considerably from one region to another although the same varieties of grapes are grown throughout the country. Different soils and climates are fundamentally responsible for the differences in German wines.

Selection procedures can also affect wine. During a vineyard's harvest, grapes of particular quality may be set aside for a special stock. A wine's label will indicate if the choice of grapes was somehow given particular attention. For example, the term *auslese* on the label of a German wine denotes it was made from specially selected bunches of grapes. An even more discriminating process is indicated by the word *beerenauslese*. This term signifies that individual grapes from select bunches were used to make the wine. Selection also affects wine by determining its sweetness. Rich, sweet wines result from grapes allowed to ripen and dry on the vine to a raisinlike sweetness before being harvested very late in the season. *Trockenbeerenauslese* on a label signifies that overripe grapes were singly selected to make the wine. Conversely, grapes for dry wines are picked earlier, before they become too sweet. Dinner table wines are of this category.

Wine is said to be supremely simple to make—just add a little yeast to the juice of crushed grapes and in a while the natural sugars will cause the mixture to ferment. Of course, that is a drastic oversimplification; control must be exercised in the fermenting process. It is not "dryness" (nonsweetness) that makes a wine tart. Tartness develops during the fermenting process. It is determined by the amount of tannic acid imparted by the skins of the grapes. The skillful winemaker can control a wine's tartness by regulating the length of time the skins remain in the fermenting juice.

When wines are categorized (as in the chart to follow) it is tempting to make comparisons that should not be made. Imported wines have been grouped with American wines from our western wine-growing region. Even though California wines are largely produced from vines originally imported from France, comparable wines from the two countries are not alike. To understand the truth of this, consider how much greater are the soil and climate differences between California and France than between the wine growing regions of Germany.

With New York State wines climatic conditions bear heavily on the varieties of grapes that can be grown. While native grape varieties such as Catawba, Delaware, and Elvira abound under local conditions, European varieties will not survive except as hybrids.[1] A New York State wine labeled "Burgundy" (referring to a French place-name wine) is not produced from the vines that produce French Burgundies, but from hybrids of French varieties. In some cases the local wine is blended with California wine of the "Burgundy" type. Labels on these bottles indicate the contents are American wine.

In either case, it is in blending more traditional wine varieties with local, native grapes that results in a wine that is decidedly different from the classic types. For these reasons, wines of the eastern United States are very difficult to fit into the scheme of European-derived varieties. Though they are popular and distinctive in their own right, they have not been included in the chart at the chapter's end.

---

[1] Vines are hybridized or crossed with another variety for many reasons: to improve hardiness in extremely cold winter climates, to increase yield, or to endow a variety with some desirable quality possessed by another. California vines too are occasionally hybridized. The Ruby Cabernet, used in making many Claret type wines, is an example of this. It is a cross between the local Carignane and the imported Cabernet Sauvignon varieties.

All these factors of grape growing and processing affect the price of the wine we buy. It is necessary to accept at the outset that good wines are somewhat expensive and compromises are usually disappointing. In almost every instance, wines are less satisfactory when purchased in bulk containers. It is an unfortunate development that the quality of wine in magnum (two-fifths of a gallon), half-gallon or gallon containers—presumably so packaged to meet an increasing demand—is often considerably inferior to other wines from the same producer. Frequently, even a good label conceals a poor wine when bottled in a large-quantity container.

The adjective, "good," when applied to wine, is usually a function of price. Often the beginner hesitates to spend much money on wine because he feels he cannot trust his judgment. Unfortunately, this type of economy often leads to a lower-quality wine. One should approach wine selection understanding that it is better to drink less of a good wine than to waste money on a poor one. Low-quality wine provides no aesthetic pleasure and spoils the food with which it is served. With that attitude in mind, it is good to know that a selection of good, moderately priced wines is available almost everywhere in this country.

Storage and Service

There are no mysteries attending wine use and service. Since fine, rare wines are seldom acquired, the problems of proper storage are of little concern to the average consumer. Rest a bottle of wine on its side. This helps to keep the cork wet and the seal tightly secure. Ideally, wine should be stored in a cool place where the temperature is fairly constant, such as in a closet or a basement.

In serving wines, temperature extremes should be avoided. Reds are best at cool room temperature (60 F or 15 C) and whites may be chilled an hour in the refrigerator before uncorking. Red wines, in particular, are enhanced by uncorking the bottle half-an-hour before dinner. Oxygen allows the flavor and fragrance of the bouquet to round out.

All wines taste better in half-filled glasses. The top half of the glass captures the bouquet, which, when inhaled, provides an important facet in the appreciation of a good wine. Avoid using wine glasses with designs that distract from an appraisal of a wine's color and clarity and *never* serve wine in metal glasses. Silver goblets may look beautiful in a table setting, but they will destroy any wine by an adverse chemical action between the two substances. The best choice is a clear glass with a large, six-ounce bowl which may be held by its stem. In this way the contents of the bowl will not be warmed by one's own body temperature.

After dinner, the wine bottle may be recorked and refrigerated. A wine loses all its bouquet once its bottle has been opened, but it will still be perfectly suitable for cooking. If it is known at the outset that only half the bottle will be consumed, it is better to decant this amount into a small carafe. Recork and refrigerate the bottle quickly and the remainder will then be drinkable the next day. Allow sufficient time for refrigerated red wine to return to cool room temperature before serving.

Wines Outside the Meal

The chart in this section deals exclusively with dry dinner wines served with the main course of a meal. There are many other kinds of wine that may be served with other courses or at other times. Sauternes, for instance, is a basic type of wine, but it is not listed on the chart. The California and the French wines of that name bear virtually no relationship to one another. French Sauternes (with a final "s") is a relatively sweet white wine, usually served with a first course of shellfish or other seafood. California Sauterne, on the other hand, ranges from semisweet to exceedingly dry.

Appetizer wines include the Sherries, dry or semisweet (Amontillado), and they are sometimes served with first-course soups, particularly thick, rich, cream soups. Flavored wines are called apéritifs. They range from wines flavored with herbs such as May wine (infused with woodruff) and the Vermouths (with several herbs) to Greek Retsina (with resin added). Spanish Sangría is flavored with the juice of other fruits. Before dinner is also a good time to serve a Rosé.

However, relying on Rosé to fulfill all wine needs impedes experimentation with wine. Aside from sautéed liver or ham, most dishes would be better accompanied by any number of red or white wines. Good Rosés include the California Grignolino, Grenache or Gamay varieties, and the French districts' Bordeaux Rosé, Burgundy Rosé or Tavel (from the Rhône Valley) and Rosé d'Anjou (of the Loire Valley).

With the exception of Champagne, sparkling wines are usually not satisfactory selections for good food. However, the New York State champagnes, made almost exclusively of native grapes, are fine complements to well-prepared food.

Unless dessert consists of cheese (in which case it is better to pour more of the dry wine served with dinner), decidedly sweet wines are best reserved for later in the meal. It confuses the palate as much to serve these wines early in the meal as it does to serve sweet dishes. They are not compatible with main course dishes, especially meats. Wine to serve with dessert, for dessert, or after a meal could be a Port, Madeira, Cream Sherry, Chateau Sauterne, Chateau Y'quem (a very sweet French Sauternes), Muscatel, Tokay, or Angelica.

White Wines

Light, delicate, "youthful" . . . serve with eggs, fish, shellfish, pork.

Full-bodied, fruity, "womanly" . . . serve with poultry, cheese, ham, beef, veal, lamb, steaks, chops, roasts.

CALIFORNIA

Rhine: Grey Riesling
Johannisberg
Riesling
Sylvaner
Traminer

FRANCE

Alsace: Riesling
Traminer
Sylvaner
Gewürtztraminer

Loire: Muscadet

ITALY

Veneto: Soave

GERMANY

Moselle: Bernkasteler
Wehlener

Riesling

CALIFORNIA

Chablis: Chenin Blanc
Le Blanc de Blancs
Pinot Chardonnay
Green Hungarian

FRANCE

Bordeaux: Graves

Burgundy: Chablis
Puligny-Montrechet
Pouilly-Fuissé
Meursault

*Rhône
Valley:* White Hermitage

ITALY

Tuscany: White Chianti

GERMANY

Rhinegau: Schloss
Johannisberger
Rauenthal

Chablis

Red Wines

Medium-bodied, "gentlemanly" . . . serve with poultry, cheese, ham, beef, veal, lamb, steaks, chops, roasts.

Full-bodied, hearty, robust . . . serve with forceful sauces, beef, lamb, mutton, venison, sausages, pastas.

CALIFORNIA

Claret: Zinfandel
         Cabernet
           Sauvignon

FRANCE

Bordeaux: Claret
           Margaux
           Saint-Émilion
           Saint-Julien
           Saint-Estèphe

Rhône
  Valley: Chateauneuf-
             du-Pape

ITALY

Veneto: Valpolicella
         Bardolino

Claret

CALIFORNIA

Burgundy: Gamay
             Beaujolais
           Pinot Noir
           Barbera

FRANCE

Burgundy: Volnay
           Beaune
           Pommard
           Beaujolais

Rhône Valley: Hermitage

ITALY

Tuscany: Chianti

Piedmont: Barbaresco
           Barolo

GERMANY

Rhinehessen: Ingelheimer

Rhinegau: Assmannhauser

Burgundy

The Dinner Wines

The first consideration in selecting a wine for the main course is the nature of the food being served, particularly the meat and accompanying sauce. Choose a wine which matches the lightness, heaviness, richness, or spiciness of the meal. Most dishes fall within a middle range—neither too mild, nor too stout—and may, therefore, be served with either white wines of defined body and flavor or red wines with lighter qualities.

Our Wine Chart* (to which the recipes in this book refer) is based on the understanding that there are four broad categories for all dry dinner wines: light whites, full whites, medium reds, and full reds. Throughout the world many single varieties of grapes are grown for dinner wines. They are placed in one of these four categories by their characteristics. Blends of wines within a category are given a "generic" name and are called a "generic wine." The generic of light, white wines is Rhine, and of full whites, Chablis. Claret is the generic name of medium red wines. The full red wines have the generic name Burgundy.

A Claret, for example, may be composed of several grape varieties such as Zinfandel, Cabernet Sauvignon, and Ruby Cabernet. These grape varieties are "related" because their wines taste fruity; they are medium-bodied and have a ruby red color. Burgundy is composed of varieties that produce a hearty, full-bodied wine with a rich warm red color. Rhine wine, one of the white generics, has lively flavor, light body, and pale gold to green gold color. The other generic white, Chablis, is blended of fragrant, fruity wines. A Chablis is fuller-bodied than the Rhine wines and has a pale golden color. Every bottle of wine we buy is a blend of more than one variety. The winemaker's art is to find the perfect combination for his winery's label; this blending accounts for one vintner's Claret being perceptibly different from another's.

Sometimes a wine is labeled with a grape variety name instead of its generic name. Zinfandel and Cabernet Sauvignon, of the Claret group, are examples of varietal wines. Because stringent regulations govern wine labeling, a California wine, for example, may be given a varietal name only if the blend is dominated by the wine of a single variety. (To be labeled "Zinfandel," 51 percent of the total mixture must be wine from the Zinfandel grape.) On the other hand, French wines are traditionally distinguished by wine growing districts: Alsace, Bordeaux, Burgundy, Rhône Valley. They along with other imported wines from Germany and Italy (also listed by districts) have been placed on the chart as they relate to the general qualities of the four basic generic wines.

With experience, the reader will discover the subtleties of origin and will learn, for instance, that American and French Beaujolais are generally similar but specifically different. Exceptions will also become apparent. A

Beaujolais, though listed properly as a Burgundy, is a reasonably light red wine; Cabernet Sauvignon, on the other hand, is hearty in comparison with the other Clarets. It is instructive to compare French and American wines of the same name or within the same generic category.

Armed with an understanding of these basics, the beginner can select wines with assured confidence by consulting the Wine Chart. However, this chart is by no means complete, and the reader should investigate further by reading about wines and tasting many different kinds.

For future reference, it is convenient to remove bottle labels (accomplished easily by a few minutes' soaking in water) and paste them in a notebook. Next to the label note responses to the wine, its qualities, and compatible foods. Eventually a preference will emerge for certain wineries (*e.g.*, for American wines) and for particular importers or shippers of the imported wines (also see Label Reading Guide).

Developing an appreciation for the centuries of care and devotion that make up our heritage of good wine and good food helps us to understand how cooking and winemaking have been elevated to the level of art. Happily for us these are arts that everyone can practice and acquire!

Label Reading Guide

The two fictitious labels, one each from a typical California and French wine, demonstrate how to evaluate the contents of a bottle. The label is quite informative and gives a good idea of what to expect from the wine inside.

Italian wines are labeled essentially like French wines. To be assured of quality, watch that an Italian wine label indicates the region of origin by name and look for the phrase, *denominazione di origine controllata*. An exceptional German wine may include *kabinett* in the name. That denotes a winemaster's special reserve.

California Wine Label

1. Winegrowing districts: Sonoma-Mendocino, Lodi, Livermore Valley-Alameda, Modesto-Ripon-Escalon, Santa Clara-San Benito, Santa Cruz-Monterrey, Fresno-San Joaquin-Kern, Cucamonga, Napa Valley.

2. Term meaning that grapes are solely from the vineyards of the winery.

3. Refers to a specific vat of wine or to all wine made at one time under similar conditions.

4. Wine name indicates that 51 percent of the wine in this bottle is from the variety, Cabernet Sauvignon. If less, it would be given the generic name, Claret.

5. "Vintage" California wine indicates all grapes were processed in the specified year.

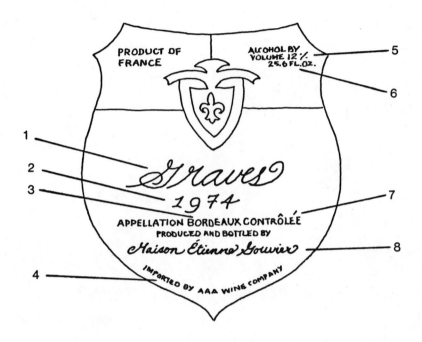

French Wine Label

1. Name of wine.

2. For French wines a "vintage" year is one in which all grapes reach full maturity.

3. Indicates the wine-growing region.

4. Name of the importer.

5. Rate for table wines. Sherries are fortified with alcohol and the percentage is higher.

6. After January 1, 1979, all wine labels will be measured in the metric equivalent. This standard size bottle is one-fifth gallon or 750 milliliters.

7. Phrase refers to legislated regulations guaranteeing the integrity of the place name, the origin of the wine, and assures upholding of standards for a given wine. Wines made collectively from the produce of small vineyards in the country are designated to be of high quality when they carry the stamp, V.D.Q.S., on the label. That mark stands for "Delimited Wines of Superior Quality."

8. Name of shipper. Without a shipper, label will read, *mis en bouteilles au Château, au Domaine,* or *à la Propriété,* all French terms for "Estate Bottled."

4

The Framework

This chapter is the foundation for a modern system of French cooking. It contains the primary dishes and develops the essential methods for preparing them. At the same time that past methods are revealed, contemporary changes are presented. This is done in stages. Just as it is easier to join two posts than to execute precisioned mortises, cooking skills are introduced in this chapter in a logically progressive manner. The first techniques are simple, yet fundamental, while later ones fill in and reinforce them.

Incorporated in the process of skill building is the demonstration of revised techniques. These new methods are viable because they rest on the age-old foundations of classic cuisine. The aim is to preserve the essential structure of the old while remodeling it to suit the culinary needs of today.

A Good Beginning:
Pot-au-Feu

This is an introductory section in the fullest sense and is designed to serve two purposes. First, the pot-au-feu is a logical starting point for developing cooking skills. It is as simple as putting the "pot on the fire." The meats are simply poached. In the process, however, the reader is introduced to stockmaking and to the French system of sauces. These are central to French cooking, traditional and modern, so it is only proper that they be used from the beginning.

Second, the pot-au-feu presents an exercise in planning. Several techniques for efficient food use are introduced in this dish. In reading through the recipes, it will become evident how the cooking of one dish may lead right to the preparation of another. In pot-au-feu, everything—meat, vegetables, herbs, and cooking liquid—is cooked together in quantity. From this basis, one may prepare several meals. The pot-au-feu recipe yields five main dishes, most of a week's cooking. The major, initial effort can be accomplished in one day and need only be augmented with vegetable or sauce preparation for the remaining four menus.

Complete menus are given in this section, but the entire book is arranged to make it easy for the reader to compose a week's menus by combining any two or three sections. The most recommended and economical way to shop is once a week with a list based on preplanned menus. In this way, seasonal or weekly advertised specials may be more efficiently utilized. For instance, if a veal roast is on sale, turn to that section, see what can be done with it, and compose the week's menus accordingly.

A shopping list is provided for the five pot-au-feu menus. But, since all recipes in the book begin with a list of ingredients, it is a simple matter to check supplies on hand against the recipes and prepare a shopping list for a week.

In all essential aspects—as an introduction to skills, as a means of showing the importance of sauces, and as a demonstration of planning methods—cooking pot-au-feu provides a basis for the subsequent sections. Those that follow will develop variations on these first steps and present other, new devices.

THE MENUS

I

Hearts of Celery, Vinaigrette
Pot-au-Feu: Beef Brisket and Vegetables,
Beef Stock, Dijon Mustard, Sour Pickles
French Bread

II

Green Salad with Sauce Vinaigrette
Chicken Mornay
Risotto   Buttered Peas

III

Slices of Beef Brisket with Horseradish Cream Sauce
Puréed Potatoes
Buttered Green Beans   Beets, Flemish Style

IV

Red Rice Salad
(Rice and beets in vinaigrette sauce with peas,
beef, green beans, Swiss cheese and hard-cooked eggs)
French Bread

V

Petite Marmite, Henri IV
Grated Swiss Cheese   French Rolls

Wine Guide. For any of these menus choose a light red Claret wine or a white Chablis or one of their varietals. See the chart in Chapter 3 to make selections.

Note. Dessert for all menus could be assorted cheeses and fruits. For suggestions see the Desserts section of the last chapter.

SHOPPING LIST

This list contains the required ingredients to execute all the dishes in this section. Consult the specific recipes to determine the exact amounts for your needs according to the number of persons to be served.

Butcher
beef brisket, 3-4 lbs. (1.5-2 kg) oxtail, if possible
few veal bones marrow bone, if desired
frying chicken, 3 lbs. (1.5 kg)

Baker
French bread, loaf
French rolls

Produce
parsley, fresh, 1 bunch carrots
celery tomatoes
celery hearts green beans
parsnips, if available peas (may be frozen)
turnips green onions or fresh chives
small onions lettuce for salads
leeks, if possible fruits for desserts
beets

Dairy
butter sour cream, small carton
eggs Swiss cheese
milk assorted cheeses for desserts
whipping cream

Seasonings and Other Supplies
salt horseradish
pepper mayonnaise
thyme flour
basil rice
nutmeg oil
whole cloves sour pickles
bay leaf canned chicken stock, if necessary
wine vinegar wine to drink
Dijon mustard

Menu One

Hearts of Celery, Vinaigrette*
Pot-au-Feu: Beef Brisket and Vegetables,
Beef Stock, Dijon Mustard, Sour Pickles,
French Bread

POT-AU-FEU

Ingredients

beef brisket	chicken
veal bones	parsnips
salt	turnips
parsley	carrots
thyme	onions
bay leaf	whole cloves
hearts of celery	leeks
butter	

A total cooking time of about 5 hours is necessary to complete the pot-au-feu.

Cook the beef. Place in a large kettle:
   3-4 lb. (1.5-2 kg) piece of beef brisket,
   a few veal bones,
   1 Tbs. (30 g) salt,
   cold water to cover.

Bring slowly to simmer, skimming off the scum as it rises to the surface. In order to keep the stock clear, always keep it at simmer; do not allow the stock to boil. When the scum ceases to rise add to the pot:
   4 sprigs parsley,
   pinch of thyme,
   ⅓ domestic bay leaf,
   2-3 hearts of celery.

Continue to simmer slowly but remove the hearts of celery when they are tender after about 40 to 60 minutes. Drain the celery hearts and chill them in the refrigerator. Serve the celery for a first course with a vinaigrette sauce.*

Preheat the oven 450 F (210 C).

Add the chicken. After the beef has simmered about 2 hours rub the skin of a
   3 lb. (1.5 kg) frying chicken with
   softened butter.

Place the buttered chicken in a roasting pan and brown it in the oven for 20 to 30 minutes. Browning the chicken gives a good color to the stock. Add the chicken to the pot.

Add the vegetables. After the chicken has been added, prepare the vegetables. Cut into neat pieces allowing 2 or 3 pieces of each vegetable per person:

> parsnips, scraped,
> turnips, peeled,
> carrots, scraped,
> small onions, peeled, the base pierced to insure even cooking,
> leeks, if available, carefully washed.

Press into each onion

> a whole clove.

Add the vegetables to the pot and simmer for about 1½ hours. All the ingredients will then be tender and ready to serve.

Serve. Remove the brisket and vegetables from the pot but leave the chicken in the stock to cool so that it will stay moist. Carve some of the beef in slices and arrange it attractively with the vegetables on a large platter. Dip out some of the stock, strain it, and skim off the fat from its surface. Serve the stock in a sauce dish with the beef and vegetables.

Notes. (1) After dinner, when the stock is cool, remove the chicken to a plate and sever the legs through the cartilage in the joint.

(2) Store the chicken legs separately in a small dish. They will be used in Menu Five.

(3) Cover the rest of the chicken and refrigerate it. This is used next in Menu Two.

(4) Transfer the stock from the kettle to a smaller container and store it *uncovered* in the refrigerator.

Variation. While this particular pot-au-feu was planned to provide several meals, a scaled-down version for a single meal can be made by browning (in 1 Tbs. [15 g] each of butter and oil) 5 to 6 short ribs of beef and odd chicken parts such as the wings and backs. Simmer the ribs in water to cover with salt, pepper, and a bouquet of herbs for an hour. Add the chicken pieces and vegetables to the pot to cook for another 1 to 1½ hours, then serve.

Menu Two

Green Salad with Sauce Vinaigrette*
Chicken Mornay
Risotto*   Buttered Peas

CHICKEN MORNAY ▰▰▰▰▰▰▰▰▰▰▰▰▰▰▰▰▰▰

Ingredients

sauce Mornay*	dry bread crumbs
chicken from the pot-au-feu	butter
Swiss cheese	

Preheat the oven 375 F (170 C).

Prepare the chicken. Reserve the legs for another menu. Remove the meat from the chicken in large pieces. Discard the skin.

Prepare the sauce. *Doubling* the amounts given (in the recipe in the section on sauces) make

2 cups (500 ml) sauce Mornay.

Assemble the dish. Butter a casserole dish and spread a thin layer of the sauce over the bottom. Arrange the chicken pieces over the sauce in the casserole. Pour the remaining sauce over the chicken. Blend together:

1 Tbs. (15 ml) grated Swiss cheese,

1 Tbs. (15 ml) fine dry bread crumbs.

Sprinkle the cheese and bread crumbs over the sauced chicken and arrange over the top

1 Tbs. (15 g) butter, cut into small pieces.

Bake the dish. Thirty minutes before serving, place the casserole in the top of the preheated oven and cook until the sauce is bubbling and the top is lightly browned.

Notes. (1) When preparing the risotto to serve with the chicken, cook *twice* the amount of rice usually required. The additional rice will be used to make the salad in Menu Four. For four persons, 1½ cups (375 ml) rice to 3 cups (750 ml) water should be sufficient for both purposes.

(2) Cook ½ to ¾ cup (125-180 ml) more peas than you plan to serve with this menu. The extra peas will also be added to the salad in Menu Four.

(3) After dinner, store the extra rice and peas in separate containers in the refrigerator.

(4) Bread crumbs are often used as a topping and as a coating for the inside of soufflé pans. Since they keep their freshness almost indefinitely, it is worth a few minutes' preparation to always have them on hand. Place a dozen slices of bread trimmed of crusts in a slow oven 200 F (80 C) until they are lightly browned and hard. Crumble the dried bread by whizzing broken pieces in a blender. Store in a covered jar in the refrigerator.

Menu Three

Slices of Beef Brisket with Horseradish Cream Sauce
Puréed Potatoes*
Buttered Green Beans* Beets, Flemish Style*

SLICES OF BEEF BRISKET, HORSERADISH CREAM SAUCE ██████████

Ingredients

beef brisket from the pot-au-feu	sour cream
stock from the pot-au-feu	horseradish
whipping cream	salt
	pepper

Prepare the sauce. Combine:
    ½ cup (125 ml) whipping cream, whipped,
    spoonful of sour cream,
    horseradish to taste,
    salt and pepper to taste.
Prepare the meat. Heat in a skillet over medium heat
    ½ cup (125 ml) stock from the pot-au-feu,
       hardened fat removed.
Add
    slices of beef brisket previously cooked in the pot-au-feu.
Leave the slices of meat in the hot stock only until they are heated through. Serve immediately accompanied with the horseradish sauce.

    Notes. (1) Arrange to have a scant ½ cup (125 ml) cooked beets and a generous cup (250 ml) cooked green beans remaining to use in the salad in Menu Four.

    (2) After dinner, cut from the remaining brisket about 1 cup (250 ml) thin julienned† pieces ¼ x ¼ x 2-inches (.5x.5x5 cm). Cover and store in the refrigerator. These beef strips will be used in the salad, Menu Four.

    (3) Remove all the hardened fat from the surface of the chilled pot-au-feu stock.

    (4) Add any remaining pieces of beef brisket to the stock along with the two legs saved from preparing the chicken. Transfer these ingredients to a freezer container and freeze. This will be used later to make a soup in Menu Five.

    (5) Combine the rice (the additional risotto saved from the Chicken Mornay dinner, Menu Two) with the ½ cup (125 ml) beets saved from Menu Three. Let them stand overnight, covered in the refrigerator. Stir them once or twice during the evening.

    (6) Store the 1-1½ cups (250-375 ml) cooked green beans reserved from Menu Three in a small, covered bowl in the refrigerator.

Menu Four

Red Rice Salad
French Bread

RED RICE SALAD ▬▬▬▬▬▬▬▬▬▬▬▬▬▬▬▬▬▬▬▬▬▬▬

Ingredients

rice and beets from Menus Two and Three, combined	parsley
julienned† strips of beef brisket, pre-prepared	dried basil
	green onions or fresh chives
green beans from Menu Three	salt
vinaigrette sauce*	pepper
peas from Menu Two	Swiss cheese
mayonnaise	hard cooked eggs

Prepare in advance. Stir the combined rice and beets several times during the day. About two hours before serving mix up a
vinaigrette sauce.*

Pour some of the sauce over the rice and beets, some of it over the julienned strips of beef, and the remainder over the green beans. Stir the contents of each container occasionally during the marinating period.

Compose the salad. Fold the peas into the red rice and beets. Blend together:

2–3 Tbs. (30-45 g) mayonnaise,
1 sprig parsley, minced,
¼ tsp. dried basil,
2 green onions, minced, or
½ tsp. fresh chives, chopped,
salt and pepper lightly to taste.

Fold the mayonnaise into the rice and vegetables. Arrange lettuce on a platter. Mound the rice-beets-peas in the center. Place in little groupings around the rice:

marinated green beans,
julienned strips of Swiss cheese,
hard-cooked eggs, quartered.

Add a cluster of parsley to garnish the rice.

Menu Five

Petite Marmite, Henri IV
Grated Swiss Cheese   French Rolls

PETITE MARMITE, HENRI IV ━━━━━━━━━━━━━━━━━━━━━━━━━━━━

Ingredients

stock from the pot-au-feu	oxtail, if available
frozen with pieces of beef	marrow bone, if desired
brisket and chicken legs	Swiss cheese
carrots	French rolls
turnip	canned chicken stock, if
leeks or onions	necessary
celery	

Prepare the stock. Defrost the beef–chicken stock by transferring it from the freezer to the refrigerator for 24 to 48 hours before preparation time. A true marmite has a doubly rich stock because pot-au-feu stock is used and a new brisket and chicken legs are simmered in it. The strength of the stock may be intensified further by boiling it down *without the meats* until it is reduced to about half. If there is not enough stock add a good quality undiluted canned stock.

Prepare the soup. Oxtail adds a great deal to the quality of the stock. If available, parboil† 10 minutes

    1 oxtail, cut up.

Drain and rinse the oxtail in cold water. Add it to the pot-au-feu stock and simmer, partially covered, for 1½ hours. Cut into sizes convenient for eating:

    2 carrots,

    1 turnip,

    2 leeks or 1 small onion quartered or a few pearl onions,

    2 stalks of celery.

Add the vegetables to the soup kettle. Skim the stock as necessary while it cooks.

Final preparation. Taste the soup for seasoning and add salt if required. Dry out in a slow oven

    sliced rounds of French rolls.

They should be lightly brown and crisp like little melba toasts. For sprinkling into the hot soup prepare

    1 cup grated Swiss cheese.

Poached marrow is sometimes served with this soup. To prepare it have a butcher split

    a marrow bone.

Carefully scoop out the marrow and cut it in a small dice. Poach it gently by simmering it in a little salted water for 1 to 2 minutes.

Serve. Place 1 to 2 slices of dried roll in the bottom of each soup plate. Ladle the soup into the bowls distributing it so that each serving has some of each meat and vegetable. Pass the cheese, extra rolls (or toasts), and poached marrow separately.

Note. Any broth remaining from the soup may be used as brown stock to make sauce Espagnole* to accompany rib roast, or as the foundation for Espagnole variations such as Madeira sauce* for ham or Bordelaise sauce* for steak.

Rump Roast of Beef

A rump roast is one of the most versatile cuts of meat. Its excellent flavor makes it the choice of many chefs for the pot-au-feu instead of a brisket. While the meats in the foregoing section were poached through a process of slow simmering in water to cover, the recipes in this section rely on the braising method for its tenderizing effect. Braised meat is also cooked in liquid (but comparatively less than for poaching) and the meat is browned in hot oil before the liquid is added.

A good rump roast may also be simply roasted† as described for the sirloin roast in the next section. Roasting is cooking in an open pan in an oven without liquid, a process sometimes known as the "dry heat" method. The roasting procedures for a sirloin or rump roast are identical and remaining meat may be utilized in the same recipes.

For the sake of functional, everyday cooking for relatively few people, the large roast has been divided. Six to ten slices, ⅜-inch (.8 cm) thick have been removed from the large end, as illustrated. You may, however, wish to prepare the entire roast, instead of just half of it, in the popular marinade–and–braise of the Beef à la Mode. To do so, exactly double all amounts for the ingredients of the marinade and braising stock. Cooking time will be longer, 3½ to 4 hours, but test for doneness by judging the tenderness of the meat when it is pierced with a fork.

Depending on how much meat is left, you may also prepare a Daube Niçoise and perhaps a Russian salad. The daube in this section is a modern adaptation which converts the remains from the Beef à la Mode to a traditional dish of smothered beef in a casserole. Dishes of this type may, of course, be made from previously uncooked meat and notes for the procedure are given after the recipe.

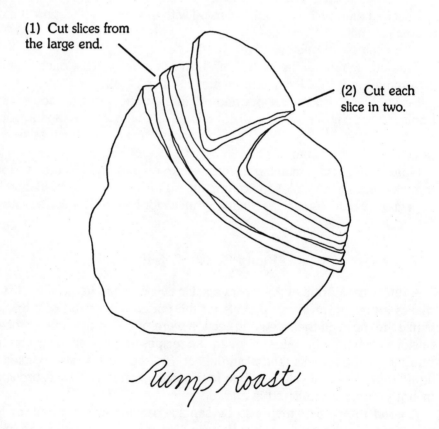

(1) Cut slices from the large end.

(2) Cut each slice in two.

Rump Roast

Beef À la Mode

Ingredients

carrot	Cognac
onion	oil
celery	dry red wine
garlic	rump roast
thyme	beef or veal bones
bay leaf	butter
parsley	flour
whole clove	brown beef stock*
salt	bacon
pepper	tomato

Prepare the marinade. Combine in a large bowl:

1 carrot, sliced,
1 onion, sliced,
1 celery stalk, sliced,
1 clove garlic, peeled, sliced,
pinch thyme,
¼ domestic bay leaf,
2 sprigs parsley,
1 whole clove,
1 tsp. (10 g) salt,
3 grinds pepper,
1 Tbs. (15 ml) Cognac,
2 Tbs. (30 ml) oil,
1 cup (250 ml) dry red wine.

Add to the bowl with the marinade

the rump roast (weighing 3-4 lbs [1½-2 kg] after slices have been
removed from the end to make beef rolls).

Marinate the meat for 6 to 24 hours, turning it now and then.
Preheat the oven 350 F (160 C).

Cook the meat. When the meat is well marinated, remove it and dry it
thoroughly on paper towels. Brown the roast in a heavy casserole over
medium-high heat in

2 Tbs. (30 ml) oil.

When the roast is brown remove it to a side dish. Add and brown

a few veal or beef bones.

Pour out the browning fat. Make a light brown roux† by adding and
cooking together:

1 Tbs. (15 g) butter,
1 Tbs. (15 g) flour.

Add to the roux stirring constantly:

the marinade ingredients,
2 cups (500 ml) beef stock.

Bring the sauce slowly to a boil, stirring now and then. Lay over the
   roast 4 to 5 pieces of bacon, blanched by simmering 10 minutes
   in 1 qt. (1 l) water; drained, rinsed, dried.
Return the roast to the casserole and add
   1 tomato, peeled, seeded, chopped.
Bring the contents of the casserole again to the simmer. Cover the
casserole and set it on a low rack in the preheated oven for 2½ to 3 hours
or until tender when pierced with a sharp fork.

Serve. Take out the meat and remove the bacon. Slice the meat and
arrange it on a platter. Dip out a cup (250 ml) of sauce. Skim off the fat
and spoon a little of the sauce over each slice of meat.

Wine Guide. Select a Burgundy or one of its varietals or Cabernet
Sauvignon. Consult the chart in Chapter 3 for specific wines from which to
choose.

DAUBE NIÇOISE

Ingredients

cooking liquid from the Beef à la Mode	black olives
	oil
basil	salt
beef previously cooked in Beef à la Mode	parsley
	large macaroni

Cook the macaroni. While preparing the sauce below, also cook the
pasta by bringing to a boil over high heat:
   2 qts. (2 l) water,
   1 tsp. (10 g) salt,
   1 Tbs. (15 ml) oil.
When the water is at a rolling boil add
   12 oz. (360 g) large macaroni.
After the water returns to a boil reduce the heat slightly so that the water
continues to boil but does not boil over. Stir the pasta now and then to
prevent its sticking to the bottom of the pan. When the macaroni is cooked
al dente† drain it into a large sieve.

Adapt the cooking liquid to a sauce. Remove any pieces of hardened
fat which formed during refrigeration from the surface of
   the cooking liquid from the Beef à la Mode.
Season with
   ½ tsp. (2 large pinches) basil.
With a fork, mash any marinade vegetables contained in the cooking
liquid.

Final Steps. Add to the hot sauce for a quick warming
   meat remaining from the Beef à la Mode cut in thick slices.
At the last minute stir in
   2 to 3 oz. (60-90 g) black olives.

Serve. Toss the cooked macaroni with a few spoonfuls of the sauce and garnish with

    2 to 3 sprigs of parsley, minced.

Wine Guide. Serve with any dry red wine.

Note. To prepare this dish from previously uncooked meat, marinate pieces of 1 to 1½ lbs. (450-675 g) stewing beef in the Beef à la Mode marinade in a heavy enameled casserole. Stir it up now and then and after 3 to 6 hours of marinating take out the meat and roll it lightly in flour. Brown the meat in hot oil. Pour out any excess oil after browning. Add to the casserole: 3 to 4 slices blanched, chopped bacon, basil, the marinade, and enough beef stock to cover the meat. Cover and cook in 325 F (150 C) oven for 3 to 4 hours until the meat is tender. Add olives, garnish, and serve as directed above.

RUSSIAN SALAD

Ingredients

    previously cooked vegetables:
      potatoes, carrots,
      green beans, peas
    mayonnaise
    salt and pepper
    julienned† strips of Beef à la Mode
    egg
    pickles
    ham and pickled tongue, optional
    pickled beets, optional

Prepare the vegetables. Combine and mix lightly:

    1 cup (250 ml) cooked, chilled, diced potatoes,
    ½ cup (125 ml) cooked, chilled, diced carrots,
    ¼ cup (65 ml) cooked, chilled green beans cut in ½-inch
      (1 cm) pieces,
    ¼ cup (65 ml) cooked, chilled peas,
    ¼ cup (65 ml) mayonnaise,
    salt and pepper to taste.

Compose the salad. Arrange the vegetables in a mound on lettuce on a platter. Garnish with:

    julienned strips of Beef à la Mode,
    hard-cooked egg, sliced,
    chopped pickles;

optional additions:

    ham and/or pickled tongue cut in julienned strips,
    pickled beets.

Wine Guide. Select a white Chablis or a red Claret or one of their varietals.

BEEF ROLLS ▬▬▬▬▬▬▬▬▬▬▬▬▬▬▬▬▬▬▬▬▬▬▬▬▬▬

Ingredients

Meat Stuffing:

onion	thyme
garlic	allspice
butter	egg
ground pork	parsley
ground veal	salt and pepper

or, *Bread Stuffing:*

butter	salt and pepper
onion	whole grain mustard
dry bread	dill pickle

Beef Rolls:

slices of beef rump roast, cut from roast before cooking	celery
	garlic
salt and pepper	thyme
string or toothpicks	bay leaf
oil or bacon fat	dry white wine
carrot	tomato paste, optional
onion	brown beef stock*

Optional Sauces:

butter	Dijon mustard
flour	cream

Prepare one of the following stuffings.

(1) *Meat Stuffing.* The meat used here may sometimes be purchased as "meat loaf mixture," or you may plan ahead to grind the meat at home. Cut a section from a veal roast and one from a pork roast, then freeze them. Time the defrosting of the stuffing meats so that they can be ground when they are still slightly crystalline. They go through most home grinders best when they are still in a partially frozen state. Cook together slowly about 5 minutes:

    1 small onion, minced,
    1 clove garlic, crushed, peeled,
    2 Tbs. (30 g) butter.

Add the onion–garlic–butter to a bowl with:

    6 oz. (180 g) medium–fat pork, ground,
    6 oz. (180 g) lean veal, ground.

Add to season:

    pinch thyme,
    dash allspice,
    salt and pepper, lightly sprinkled.

Blend in:

    1 egg,
    1 or 2 sprigs parsley, minced.

Beat together very well until thoroughly combined.

(2) *Bread Stuffing.* Cook together slowly 8 or 9 minutes:

    1 small onion, minced,

    3 Tbs. (45 g) butter.

Stir the butter and onions into a bowl with:

    dry bread,

    salt and pepper, lightly sprinkled,

    1 Tbs. whole grain mustard, or to taste,

    2 Tbs. minced dill pickle, or to taste.

Prepare the meat. Use the 6 to 10 slices cut ⅜-inch (.8 cm) thick from the widest end of a boned rump roast. Divide each of the slices in two (as illustrated). Lightly pound each of the 12 to 20 pieces with a mallet, one at a time, between 2 sheets of waxed paper. When the meat slices have been flattened to ⅓ their original thickness, season them lightly with

    salt and pepper.

Preheat the oven 325 F (150 C).

Make the rolls. Spread the stuffing on the lower half of each beef slice. Roll up jelly-roll fashion and tie with string an inch from both ends or secure with toothpicks. Dry them well on paper towels. Brown the rolls in a heavy skillet or casserole over medium-high heat in

    2 Tbs. (30 g) hot, but not smoking, bacon fat or oil.

When the rolls are well-browned on all sides, remove them to a side dish. Stir in and cook gently for 4 to 5 minutes:

    1 medium carrot, sliced,

    1 small onion, sliced.

Add a bouquet of herbs:

    1 stalk celery,

    1 clove garlic, unpeeled,

    pinch thyme,

    ¼ domestic bay leaf,

    4 sprigs parsley.

Pour in, stirring to blend:

    ½ cup (125 ml) dry white wine,

    1 tsp. tomato paste, optional.

Simmer a minute and return the beef rolls to the casserole. Pour in to nearly cover the rolls

    beef stock.

Cook the beef rolls. Heat the casserole to simmering on top of the stove. Cover it and transfer to a preheated oven to cook slowly for 1½ hours. When the rolls are tender lift them out onto a plate and remove their fastenings. Remove the herbs from the cooking stock and boil it down to about 1½ cups (375 ml) to concentrate its flavor.

Make one of the following sauces.

(1) *Sauce Simple.* Mash the vegetables which cooked with the rolls into the stock. Taste and season with salt, if necessary.

(2) *Brown Sauce.* Strain the vegetables out of the stock and discard them. Make a roux by cooking together, stirring, until nut-brown:

    1 Tbs. (15 g) butter,
    1 Tbs. (15 g) flour.

Pour in the hot stock, stirring with a wire whip to smooth. Boil to reduce slightly. Season to taste with salt.

(3) *Brown Sauce with Cream.* To the brown sauce prepared above add:

    1 Tbs. Dijon mustard,
    ⅓ cup (80 ml) cream.

Simmer to blend flavors and taste for seasoning with salt.

Wine Guide: Select a dry red wine.

Note. This is a dish that may be prepared as much as a day ahead. Transfer the cooked rolls to a clean casserole; spoon the sauce over them. Refrigerate when cool. When ready to serve, reheat carefully on top of the stove.

Beef Sirloin Roast

Roasting, one of the most important cooking methods, is often done incorrectly by the uninformed cook. When roasted meat is properly cooked—seared and finished in an *open* pan—the result will be a succulent roast with all of its juices sealed in. If meat is covered at any time while roasting, the juices will escape from the meat. Those who use these juices in making gravy should try French method pan sauces. Add water, stock, or wine to the crusty, browned drippings after the meat is removed from the pan. The pan sauce may be thickened with a roux† or not, to suit the occasion.

The Belgian Beef Stew in this section is an adaptation of the traditional recipe converted to utilize previously roasted beef. Since the original roast is of unspecified size a third recipe for Italian Meatballs is included. If sufficient meat remains this will extend the roast for another meal.

ROAST SIRLOIN OF BEEF ■■■■■■■■■■■■■■■■■■■■■■■■■■■■■■

Ingredients

beef sirloin roast	butter, optional
salt and pepper	brown beef stock,* optional
bacon	

Preheat the oven 450 F (210 C).

Prepare the meat. Season the roast lightly with
    salt and pepper.

Because this cut is very lean it should be protected from drying during

most of the roasting time. Tie around the roast
> 5 slices of fat bacon simmered 10 minutes in 1 qt. (1 l) water; drained, rinsed, and dried.

Roast the meat. Place in a shallow roasting pan and roast in a hot oven for 20 minutes. Reset the oven to 350 F (160 C) and continue to roast for 20 minutes per pound until medium-rare. Twenty minutes before the roast is done, remove the slices of fat in order to allow the meat to brown. The timing given above is for a boned roast; an unboned roast requires about half as much cooking time.

Make a pan deglazing sauce. Remove the roast from the roasting pan onto a hot platter. Carefully pour out all the fat from the roasting pan but retain any juices and browned bits. Pour in
> 1 cup (250 ml) water or beef stock.

Cook and stir to incorporate all the crusty pieces in the pan. Raise the heat and boil down rapidly to reduce the stock to a good color and flavor. Correct the seasoning, if necessary, with
> salt and pepper.

Add to the sauce any juices which may have seeped from the roast. Swirl in
> 1 Tbs. (15 g) butter, optional.

Ladle a spoonful of sauce over each slice of roast as it is served.

Wine Guide. Select a Claret or one of its varietals or a Beaujolais.

BEEF STEW, BELGIAN STYLE

Ingredients

oil	bay leaf
beef bones	thyme
onions	butter
salt and pepper	light brown sugar
garlic	wine vinegar
brown beef stock*	previously roasted beef sirloin
beer	flour
parsley	

Preheat the oven 325 F (150 C).

Prepare the sauce. Heat in a heavy casserole over medium-high heat until almost smoking
> 1-2 Tbs. (15-30 g) oil.

Brown in the hot oil
> 1 lb. (450 g) beef bones, cracked.

When well-browned, remove the bones; reduce the heat to moderate. Stir in and cook until lightly browned
> 2 medium onions, sliced.

Remove from the heat. Stir in to season:
   salt and pepper, lightly sprinkled,
   1 large clove garlic, crushed, peeled.
Add:
   1 cup (250 ml) beef stock, including any pan sauce remaining from
      previous roasting,
   3 sprigs parsley,
   ¼ domestic bay leaf,
   pinch thyme.
Return the casserole to the heat and scrape the pan to incorporate any
browned juices. Return the browned bones to the casserole, cover, and
cook in the preheated oven for 2 hours.

Prepare the meat. Cut into 2x3-inch (5x7.5 cm) pieces
   1 lb. (450 g) cold, roasted, sirloin.
Dry the pieces well; sprinkle them lightly with
   flour.
Sauté the pieces of meat very quickly in
   ½ Tbs. each (15 g total) butter and oil.
To hasten the browning and to complement the flavor of the stew,
sprinkle over the meat
   2 tsp. (15 g) light brown sugar.
Sauté only to lightly brown the flour coating; overcooking will toughen
the meat.

Final steps. Remove the casserole from the oven. Remove the bones
and herbs. Deglaze the skillet in which the meat was browned with:
   ½ cup (125 ml) water mixed with
   2 tsp. (10 ml) wine vinegar.
Add the vinegar and water to the casserole. Heat the contents of the
casserole to simmering and season lightly, if necessary, with
   salt and pepper.
Add the browned meat to the casserole. Heat again to simmering. Serve
immediately with boiled potatoes or buttered noodles.

Wine Guide. Select a Chablis or one of its varietals or any dry red wine.

Note. To prepare this dish from previously uncooked meat, brown 1 to
1¼ lbs. (450 g) stewing beef with the bones. Proceed with the recipe.

ITALIAN MEATBALLS AND ZUCCHINI

Ingredients

roasted beef	oil	salt and pepper
Italian sausage	zucchini	celery
bread	flour	parsley
milk	onion	thyme
egg	garlic	bay leaf
butter	tomatoes	

Preheat the oven 350 F (160 C).

Make the meatballs: Combine in a bowl:

1¾ cups (210 g) roasted beef, ground,

2 oz. (60 g) hot Italian sausage, casing removed,

2 slices of bread, crusts removed, soaked in

½ cup (125 ml) milk and squeezed dry,

1 egg, beaten.

Beat the mixture together until thoroughly blended. Shape into 8 balls, transfer to a plate, and chill for an hour or more until firm. After the meatballs have chilled, melt together in a heavy skillet over medium-high heat:

2 Tbs. (30 g) butter,

2 Tbs. (30 g) oil.

After the butter foams and begins to subside, add the meatballs and brown them on all sides. Transfer the meatballs to a plate.

Prepare the zucchini. Add to the browning fat in the skillet:

6 medium zucchini, peeled, thickly sliced, sprinkled and tossed with

2 Tbs. (30 g) flour.

Brown the zucchini lightly on both sides. Lift the zucchini onto a casserole with a slotted spoon. Pour out all but a spoonful of browning fat from the skillet. Stir in:

½ small onion, chopped,

1 clove garlic, crushed, peeled.

Cook and stir until the onion is transparent; then add

2 tomatoes, peeled, seeded, juiced, chopped.

Cook the tomatoes for 2-3 minutes until reduced a little. Add this tomato sauce to the zucchini in the casserole. Season the vegetables lightly with

salt and pepper.

Add a bouquet of herbs:

1 celery stalk,

3 sprigs parsley,

pinch thyme,

¼ domestic bay leaf.

Arrange the meatballs over the top of the vegetables. Cover and bake in preheated oven for 30 minutes. Remove the herbs before serving.

Wine Guide. Select a Chablis or a Claret or one of their varietals.

Variation. Substitute cooked lamb and fresh pork sausage to make the meatballs, and use eggplant instead of zucchini.

Beef Round Bone Roast

It is a special achievement of French cuisine that even the humbler cuts of beef gain distinction through appropriate preparation. The beef pot

Divide in half.

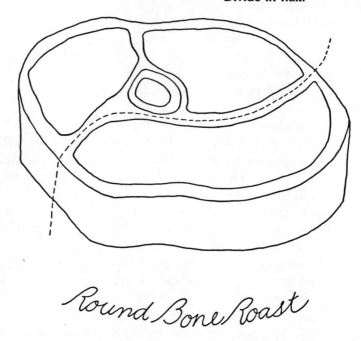

Round Bone Roast

roast to follow is just such a recipe. In contrast to Beef à la Mode (which was first marinated and then braised† in red wine), beef pot roast is cooked in white wine without previous marination.

The pot roast is prepared from approximately half of a 2½ lb. (1.25 kg) roast and the remainder is used for hachis. The latter, an informal beef hash, is prepared in a braise with stock only. It can be used as the basis for beef pies or beneath a blanket of duchess potatoes. Hachis also utilizes beef which has been simmered to make stock.*

Suggestions at the end of the section for using braised beef apply well to lamb and veal and, to a more limited extent, to pork and chicken. Exact proportions are open to experimentation and vary according to personal taste.

BEEF POT ROAST BRAISED IN WHITE WINE ▮▬▬▬▬▬▬▬▬▬▬▬

Ingredients

lean salt pork	parsley
beef round bone roast	bay leaf
oil	thyme
onions	brown beef stock*
carrots	mushrooms
salt and pepper	butter
beef or veal bones	flour
dry white wine	

Preheat the oven 350 F (160 C).

Preliminary steps. Simmer for 5 minutes

    4 oz. (120 g) lean salt pork in a quart (1 liter) of water.

Cut the pork in a dice and sauté it in a heavy skillet until lightly browned in

    1 Tbs. (15 ml) oil.

Remove the pork with a slotted spoon into a heavy casserole. Add to the skillet:

    1 medium onion, sliced,

    1 large carrot, sliced.

Lightly brown the vegetables and add them to the casserole.

Prepare the meat. Brown in the fat in the skillet adding more oil if necessary:

    round bone roast of beef, about 2½ lbs. (1.25 kg) (see illustration),

        well dried on paper towels.

When browned on both sides, place the roast in the casserole over the vegetables. Season it lightly with

    salt and pepper.

To improve the character of the stock add to the casserole

    a few beef or veal bones.

Pour out all the fat from the sauté skillet. Pour in and simmer, scraping to deglaze the pan,

    1 cup (250 ml) dry white wine.

Pour the wine and pan juices over the meat in the casserole. Add a bouquet of herbs:

    3 sprigs parsley,

    ⅓ domestic bay leaf,

    pinch thyme.

Pour in

    enough beef stock to cover two-thirds of the roast.

Braise the roast. Cover the casserole and cook about 3 hours in a preheated oven. Baste the roast frequently during this time.

Add the vegetables. During the last hour of cooking place in the casserole to finish cooking with the roast:

    small carrots, peeled and lightly browned in butter,

    small onions, peeled, lightly browned in butter,

    whole mushrooms, lightly sautéed in butter and oil.

Complete the sauce. When the meat is done and the vegetables tender, remove them from the casserole and arrange on a hot platter. Pour the stock through a strainer into a bowl. Remove the pork dice and add it to the platter. Discard bones and herbs. Skim the fat from the stock and rub the strained vegetables through the sieve into the stock to make a simple sauce. If a thicker sauce is desired add the stock and sieved vegetables to a light brown roux† of:

    1 Tbs. (15 g) butter,

    1 Tbs. (15 g) flour.

Cook until lightly thickened. Spoon some of the sauce over the roast and vegetables on the platter and serve the rest separately.

Wine Guide. Select a white Chablis or a red Claret or one of their varietals.

BEEF HACHIS ██

Ingredients

beef roast	carrot
oil	onion
celery	butter
thyme	flour
bay leaf	tomato paste, optional
parsley	pastry* or duchess potatoes*
salt	

Preheat the oven 375 F (170 C).

Prepare the meat. Divide as illustrated
 1¼ lb. (560 g) beef round bone roast cut in 2-inch cubes (5 cm cubed) and dried on paper towels.

Brown the meat over medium-high heat in
 2 Tbs. (30 ml) cooking oil.

Remove the meat to a side dish and pour out the cooking oil. Pour into the pan
 2 cups (500 ml) hot water.

Bring the water quickly to boil, stirring through to the bottom of the pan to incorporate pan drippings. Add a bouquet of herbs:
 1 stalk celery,
 pinch thyme,
 ¼ domestic bay leaf,
 3 sprigs parsley.

To season add:
 1 tsp. (10 g) salt,
 1 carrot, peeled, quartered,
 1 small onion peeled, quartered.

Cook the meat. Return the meat to the pan and bring the contents to simmer. Cook slowly 2½ to 3 hours until the meat is very tender.

Finish the sauce. If the meat has already been cooked as, for instance, in stockmaking, begin at this point (see note below). Strain out the stock. Make a roux by browning together:
 1 Tbs. (15 g) butter,
 1 Tbs. (15 g) flour.

Pour in the hot stock whisking to smooth. Blend in
 1 tsp. tomato paste, optional.

Complete the dish. Combine this sauce with the meat and transfer it to either:

> a prepared, unbaked pie shell* or,
>
> a casserole dish, piped with a decorative border of duchess potatoes.*

Bake in preheated oven until browned.

Wine Guide. Select a Chablis or Claret or one of their varietals.

Note. If the meat in this dish has been used to make stock, remove it after it has simmered in the stock for 2½ hours along with 1½ cups (375 ml) of stock. Proceed with making the roux, above.

SERVING SUGGESTIONS FOR BRAISED MEATS

Some standby methods for using previously cooked meat are listed below. They are proven menu-stretchers and are adaptable to many kinds of meats and poultry.

(1) *Cold cuts.* Simply slice and serve cold in sandwiches or with a pungent sauce on an hors d'oeuvre tray.

(2) *Salads.* Combine meats with cold, cooked vegetables and a suitable sauce, hard-boiled eggs, and cheeses. Consult the Index for salad suggestions in other sections.

(3) *Spreads.* Grind and combine with chopped, hard-boiled egg, mayonnaise thinned with cream, seasonings ranging from herbs, mustard, and pickles to dried fruits or nuts depending on the type of meat. Use as sandwich fillers and as an hors d'oeuvre spread for canapés and crackers.

(4) *Meat loaves.* Grind the cooked meat and combine it with ground, uncooked, medium-fat meat such as pork (preferably unseasoned). Mix 3 parts cooked meat to 1 part uncooked. Beat in 1 or 2 eggs and an onion sautéed in butter. Ground, cooked rice or bread soaked in milk and squeezed dry may also be added. Pack the mixture in a loaf pan. Place the loaf pan in a larger pan filled with enough boiling water to come up 1-inch (2.5 cm) on the outside of the loaf pan. Lay a sheet of aluminum foil loosely, with edges extended, over the top of the meat loaf pan and steam in a 350 F (160 C) oven for about 1 hour. Serve on a platter with an appropriate sauce.

(5) *Vegetable stuffings.* Ground or diced cooked meats may be combined according to the outline found in the chapter on vegetables.

(6) *Insulated reheating.* Cooked meat is always best reheated underneath a pastry shell or puréed potatoes as described above. Or, the shield against excessive heat may be a sauce as in the method used for croquettes.* Other examples of this technique would be the Pasta Fazool* or Cassoulet* where beans act as an insulator. Salmon with Macaroni* is a dish that could easily be adapted to beef or chicken. Sliced eggplant, zucchini, potatoes, or squares of polenta* are also effective insulator substitutes.

(7) *Fricadelles* is another insulated reheat. Make patties of diced meat and puréed potatoes. Bind with a beaten egg. Coat the patties lightly with flour and sauté them in butter and oil.

(8) *Standard hash.* In a buttered casserole place in alternate layers: (a) ground, cooked meat blended with thickened pan sauce (gravy); (b) diced onion sautéed in butter; (c) sliced potatoes. End with a layer of potatoes on top. Whip ½ cup (125 ml) heavy cream and spread over the top. Bake 350 F (160 C) for 1 hour. Herbs may be added to the cream and other vegetables could be included.

Prime Rib Roast of Beef

Because of its superior status, a prime rib roast should be served with a special sauce. Therefore, while a pan sauce could be made according to the method outlined for roast sirloin, the more complex sauce Espagnole would be a better choice. This also provides the base for the sauce variations in the two follow-up recipes. With the addition of mushrooms and cream it becomes sauce Parisienne, and with shallot and pepper, sauce Diable.

ROAST PRIME RIBS OF BEEF ▉▉▉▉▉▉▉▉▉▉▉▉▉▉▉▉▉▉▉▉▉▉▉▉▉▉▉▉▉▉ . ▉▉▉▉

Ingredients

> prime rib roast of beef
> salt and pepper
> sauce Espagnole*

Preheat the oven 450 F (210 C).

There are approximately two servings per rib and the cooking method remains the same even for a roast of 4 or 5 ribs.

Roast the meat. Lightly season a well-trimmed
> 3-rib roast of beef with
> salt and pepper.

Set it in a roasting pan, fat side up, resting on its bones. Place it in the preheated oven to sear for 20 minutes. Reduce the heat to 350 F (160 C) and roast until medium-rare counting about 12 minutes per pound (450 g). Allow the roast to rest 20 minutes after removing from the oven before carving.

Prepare the sauce. Pour out all the fat from the roasting pan. Add
> ½ to 1 cup (125-250 ml) water.

Cook down rapidly, stirring to incorporate all the drippings from the roasting pan. Add this deglazing liquid to
> 2 to 2½ cups (500–625 ml) sauce Espagnole.

Simmer a few minutes to blend the flavors.

Serve. Ladle 1 or 2 spoonfuls of the sauce over each serving of the roast.

Wine Guide. Select a Claret or one of its varietals or a Beaujolais.

SLICES OF BEEF, PARISIAN STYLE ▐███████████████████████▌

Ingredients

slices of roasted beef	Madeira
salt and pepper	sauce Espagnole*
mushrooms	cream

Prepare the mushrooms. Sauté† until lightly browned:
> ½ lb. (240 g) mushrooms, sliced, in
> 2 Tbs. (30 g) butter,
> 1 Tbs. (15 ml) oil.

Make the sauce Parisienne. Pour into the skillet of sautéed mushrooms
> 2 Tbs. (30 ml) Madeira.

Add and heat thoroughly
> 1 cup (250 ml) sauce Espagnole.

Pour in, stirring to blend
> ½ cup (125 ml) cream.

Heat the sauce to simmering.

Complete the dish. At the last minute before serving fold into the sauce the remains of the rib roast cut in cross-grained strips of uniform size and seasoned lightly with
> salt and pepper.

Heat the meat through but do not cook it any further.

Serve. Accompany the dish with risotto* or sautéed potatoes.*

Wine Guide. Select a Chablis or a Claret or one of their varietals.

RIBS OF BEEF DIABLE ▐███████████████████▌

Ingredients

roasted ribs of beef	dry white wine
Dijon mustard sauce*	sauce Espagnole*
fresh bread, crumbed	pepper
butter	parsley
green onions or shallot	

Prepare the ribs for broiling. A choice or prime grade roast will have a substantial amount of meat on three sides of each rib. Allow one rib per serving or freeze ribs until you have collected a sufficient number. Cut between each rib to separate them. Coat the pieces with
> Dijon mustard sauce.

Spread on a plate
> 1 cup (250 ml) fresh bread crumbs.

Roll each coated rib in crumbs and pat the crumbs into the mustard sauce so that they will adhere. Place the prepared ribs on an oiled broiler

rack and drizzle over them
        melted butter.
  Prepare the sauce Diable. Cook together slowly:
    1 Tbs. (15 g) butter,
    1 large green onion or shallot, minced.
  Add and boil down to reduce to half
    ¼ cup (60 ml) dry white wine.
  Blend in
    ½ cup (125 ml) sauce Espagnole.
  Season with:
      several grinds of black pepper (enough to make the sauce spicy),
      1 sprig parsley, minced.
  Broil the ribs. Place the rack 6 inches (15 cm) from the source of heat.
Turn the ribs every 2 to 3 minutes until the crumbs are nicely browned.
  Serve. Ladle 1 or 2 spoonfuls of sauce over each serving.
  Wine Guide. Choose a Burgundy or one of its varietals.

ALTERNATE PROCEDURE

Planning Note. A rib roast may be considered as much an "economy cut" as a round bone or chuck roast if it is fully utilized. In this section three main dishes have been obtained from one roast, but it can be stretched even further under an alternate plan. For instance, after the roast is cooked, all the remaining meat may be cut from the bones. About one cup (250 ml) of the most solid pieces, cut in a dice, could be used in a beef and potato or rice salad.* Grind all the remaining meat. Combine some with ground pork or sausage for a meat loaf.* Brown the bones with another small soup bone or chicken parts to make a stock for onion soup.* Later, serve some of the soup as a first course to another meal. You may combine the remaining ground beef roast with diced potatoes. Pour over the remaining onion soup and bake a savory, old-fashioned hash. Or, grind some meat from the stock bones and combine with a chopped egg, mayonnaise and seasonings. This makes about a cup of hors d'oeuvre meat spread to serve with crackers.

  Note. To braise a boneless filet roast of beef see the note at the conclusion of the recipe for Boneless Roast of Pork.*

Porterhouse Steaks

Proficiency in meat preparation is crucial to good cooking. The meat dish is the most important part of the meal. It is true, however, that Americans eat far more meat than necessary. Our enormous butter-tender beef steaks, the most excellent in the world, can easily provide many portions. Given a few tricks, good beef need not be so costly—either to the pocketbook or to the waistline.

The following recipes call for very large porterhouse steaks with generous filet sections. Order them cut 2 inches (5 cm) thick. Following the illustration, remove the filet sections and freeze them. These will be used to make the Sauté of Beef. Cut away the bones from the steaks and freeze them for stockmaking. The remaining strip sections may each serve two persons.

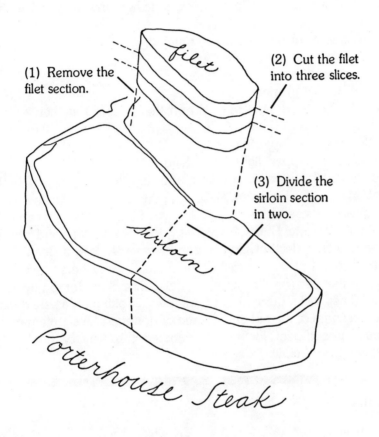

(1) Remove the filet section.

(2) Cut the filet into three slices.

(3) Divide the sirloin section in two.

filet

sirloin

Porterhouse Steak

BROILED SIRLOIN STEAKS

Ingredients

strip sections of porterhouse steaks	salt
melted butter	composed butter (see below)

Preheat the broiler for 15 minutes.
Prepare the steaks. Brush both sides of:
   beef strip steaks with
   melted butter.

Cook the steaks. Broil the first side and before turning, sprinkle the cooked side with
> salt.

For rare steaks broil 2-inch (5 cm) steaks for 10 minutes on each side. Allow slightly longer for medium-rare. Remove onto hot plates and spread with one of the following composed butters.

(1) Marchand de Vin Butter. Boil together until reduced to 3 or 4 Tbs.:
> 4 shallots or green onions, minced,
> ¾ cup (180 ml) dry red wine.

Stir in, if available
> ½ Tbs. (8 g) meat jelly.*

Allow the reduced wine to cool and then cream together:
> ¼ cup (60 g) butter,
> 2 sprigs parsley, minced,
> salt and pepper, lightly sprinkled.

Add the shallots and wine a little at a time to the creamed butter.

(2) *Variation.* Bercy Butter. Substitute dry white wine for the red in the recipe above. Also see the

(3) Maitre d'Hotel Butter,* which is good for all steaks and chops.

Wine Guide. Select a Claret or one of its varietals or a Beaujolais.

Note. Instead of oven broiling, beef steaks may be successfully prepared by the pan broiling method fully described for Sautéed Lamb Chops.* They will require about 6 minutes' cooking on a side depending on the thickness of the cut and degree of doneness. A simple pan deglazing sauce is sufficient for steaks prepared this way or use the sauce Bordelaise given below.

SAUTÉ OF BEEF

Ingredients

tomato sauce*	dry white wine
filet of beef	black olives
butter	parsley
oil	other fresh herbs, if available

Make in advance
> tomato sauce.

Prepare the meat. Following the illustration, cut
> filet sections of 2 porterhouse steaks across the grain for slices about ½-inch (1 cm) thick.

This is easily accomplished if the meat is frozen to a slightly crystalline state. Remove any fat or filament from around the slices and dry them well on paper towels.

Sauté the meat. In a heavy skillet heat together over medium-high heat:

> 1 Tbs. (15 g) butter,
> 1 Tbs. (15 g) oil.

At the point when the butter foams up and then begins to subside, add the filet slices a few at a time to the skillet. Cook them only 2 or 3 minutes on each side and remove them to a side dish when done. The interior should remain medium-rare.

Make the sauce. Pour out the sauté fat and pour in to deglaze† the skillet

> ⅓ cup (80 ml) dry white wine.

Boil rapidly to reduce to about 2 Tbs. while scraping the skillet to incorporate pan juices. Add to the skillet

> 1 cup (250 ml) tomato sauce.

Simmer a few minutes to blend the flavors. Return the beef slices very briefly for a warm-up, but carefully avoid further cooking. Garnish with:

> ½ cup (125 ml) black olives, pitted,
> 2 sprigs parsley, minced,
> other fresh herbs, if available, chopped.

Serve with sautéed potatoes,* risotto,* or buttered fettucini.

Wine Guide. Select a Chablis or one of its varietals or a light Burgundy, such as Beaujolais.

Variations. (1) *Beef Sauté, Parisian Style.* Sauté the filet slices as directed above. Pour out the sauté fat and deglaze† the pan with

> ¼ cup (60 ml) Madeira.

Stir in and simmer to blend the flavors

> 1 cup (250 ml) sauce Espagnole.*

Fold in:

> ½ cup (125 ml) cream,
> ¼ lb. (120 g) mushrooms, previously sautéed to light brown,*
> 1 or 2 minced shallots may also be stirred into the mushrooms just
> before they finish browning.

Return the meat for a brief warming and serve at once.

(2) *Beef Sauté, Bordelaise.* Sauté the slices of beef filet as directed above. Pour out all but 1 Tbs. of the sauté fat. Stir in and cook a moment

> 1 large shallot or green onion, minced.

Deglaze† the pan with

> ½ cup (125 ml) dry red wine.

Boil to reduce to 3 Tbs. Blend in

> 1 cup (250 ml) sauce Espagnole.*

Simmer about 5 minutes to combine flavors. In a small pan of simmering, salted water gently poach for 1 to 2 minutes

> the marrow from a split marrow bone cut in a small dice.

Just before serving, stir into the brown sauce and red wine:
 2 Tbs. (30 g) poached marrow,
 2 sprigs parsley, chopped.
Reheat the sautéed beef slices and serve at once.

Veal Shoulder Clod Roast

For the recipes in this section select a 3 lb. (1.5 kg) boneless roast of veal. The shoulder clod is the recommended choice. About 1 lb. (450 g) should be removed from the large end of the roast and frozen for later use as "scallops" (small, round, thin slices). Much smaller in diameter than the corresponding cut of beef, slices from the veal shoulder clod are a perfect size and weight for scallops. Furthermore, veal shoulder is tender enough to benefit from the quick sauté method. The slices could also be flattened, stuffed as described for Beef Rolls,* and braised.

The major portion of the roast will be casserole-braised, but because veal is cooked to well-done it poses a problem for secondary dishes. It must be reheated with great care. In this section, meat remaining from the

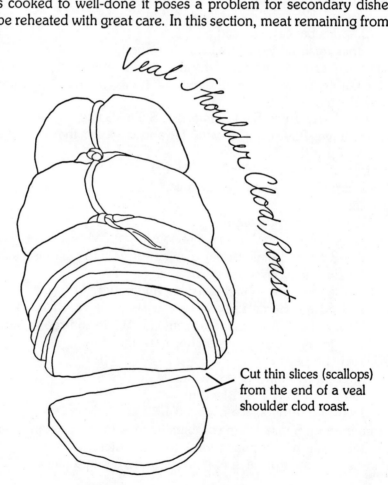

Cut thin slices (scallops) from the end of a veal shoulder clod roast.

cooked roast is used in a composed salad and in croquettes where a very heavy béchamel sauce protects the meat during reheating. Previously cooked veal could also be ground and shaped into meatballs as described in the section on Roast Sirloin of Beef.*

BRAISED ROAST OF VEAL ████████████████████████████████

Ingredients

veal roast, boneless	stock or water
butter	celery
salt and pepper	thyme
onion	bay leaf
carrot	parsley
veal bones	dry white wine

Preheat the oven 425 F (200 C).

Prepare the meat. Melt in a small skillet

    2 Tbs. (30 g) butter.

Spread the melted butter over

    2 lb. (1 kg) boneless roast of veal (this is the approximate weight after slices have been removed from the large end.

Season the roast with

    salt and pepper.

Place the veal in a casserole on a bed of vegetables:

    1 onion, peeled, sliced,

    1 carrot, scraped, sliced.

Also add

    veal bones, as available.

Sear the meat uncovered in the preheated oven for 25 to 30 minutes until golden in color. Pour into the casserole

    1 cup (250 ml) stock or water.

Add a bouquet of herbs:

    1 stalk celery,

    pinch thyme,

    ¼ domestic bay leaf,

    4 sprigs parsley.

Lay over the roast a piece of buttered brown paper cut the shape and size of the inside of the casserole (draw around the lid for a pattern; cut ½-inch or 1 cm smaller all around). Puncture the paper with a tiny hole in the middle to vent steam.

Braise the roast. Cover the casserole; reduce the oven temperature to 375 F (170 C) and cook for 1¼ to 1½ hours, basting occasionally. Test for doneness near the end of the cooking time: when the roast is deeply pricked the juices will run clear yellow.

Make the sauce. Strain off the braising liquid and skim the fat from it.

Return the liquid to the casserole with:

> 2 Tbs. (30 ml) dry white wine,

> water or stock to equal a little more than 1 cup (250 ml) liquid in all.

Boil the liquid, scraping up all the brownings from the sides and bottom of the casserole. The roast may be sliced and returned to the casserole to be reheated just before serving.

Serve. Ladle a spoonful of sauce over each serving and reserve the remaining sauce for the dishes which follow.

Wine Guide. Select a Chablis or a Claret or one of their varietals.

Variation. The last hour of braising add to the casserole and baste with the cooking stock 2 or 3 times:

> 1 tomato, peeled, seeded, chopped,

> 8 to 10 small carrots, scraped,

> 2 artichokes, stemmed, quartered, with choke and leaf tips removed.

Note. Veal chops and steaks are prepared similarly to braising a roast. Chops are browned on both sides in the casserole in a small amount of butter and oil. As they are browned, remove them to a side dish and continue until all are browned. Then add the sliced carrot and onion and cook a moment. Deglaze† the pan with ½ cup (125 ml) dry white wine or stock. Add a bouquet of herbs.† Lightly salt and pepper the chops and return them to the casserole, overlapping them as necessary to accommodate all the chops in one layer. Cover the casserole and cook in a 325 F (150 C) oven for 20 minutes, basting twice.

VEAL SALAD, PARISIAN STYLE

Ingredients

potatoes	oil
pan sauce† from roasted veal or brown beef stock*	vinaigrette sauce*
	veal, previously cooked
shallot or green onion	mild red onion
parsley	green beans, previously cooked
eggs	
wine vinegar	Boston lettuce
Dijon mustard	tomatoes
salt and pepper	fresh green herbs, if available

Make a French potato salad. Boil in salted water to cover until tender when pierced with a knife

> 4-5 medium boiling potatoes, scrubbed but not peeled.

Drain the potatoes when cooked and drop them into cold water for a moment. Peel them as soon as they can be held. Slice the hot potatoes thinly into:

> 2 Tbs. (30 ml) pan sauce from the preceding roast or beef stock,

> 1 large shallot or green onion, minced,

> 1 sprig parsley, minced.

Stir gently until the potatoes have absorbed the liquid.

Make the sauce. For a mayonnaise-like version of a vinaigrette sauce, press through a fine sieve

yolks of 2 hard-boiled eggs.

Blend into the yolks making a smooth paste:

1 Tbs. (15 ml) wine vinegar,
½ tsp. Dijon mustard, or to taste,
½ tsp. (5 g) salt,
several grinds of pepper, to taste.

Measure

3 Tbs. (45 ml) oil.

Drop by drop, beat the oil into the egg yolk paste. Fold the sauce into the warm potatoes. Set the potato salad aside to wait at cool room temperature while completing the salad (but if it is a very hot day, set the salad in the refrigerator).

Marinate the other salad elements. Using half the given amounts mix up a

vinaigrette sauce.*

Marinate in separate dishes for about ½ hour:

braised veal, thinly sliced,
rings of mild red onion,
green beans, cooked.

Serve. Arrange the potato salad, marinated veal, green beans and onion rings attractively on a platter with:

Boston lettuce,
tomatoes, quartered,
whites of hard-boiled eggs, julienned.†

Garnish with a mixture of

fresh green herbs, minced, if available or use parsley only.

Wine Guide. Serve a Chablis, a Claret, or one of their varietals.

Veal Croquettes ▬▬▬▬▬▬▬▬▬▬▬▬▬▬

Ingredients

butter	eggs
onion	veal, previously cooked
milk	oil
flour	fresh bread, crumbed
salt and pepper	deep fat for frying
paprika	

Make the sauce. In croquettes the meat is bound by enough béchamel sauce to make it very thick and heavy. In this case the veal is complemented by the paprika version of béchamel. Cook together slowly in a saucepan:

5 Tbs. (75 g) butter,
½ medium onion, finely diced.

Set to boiling in another saucepan
    2 cups (500 ml) milk.
When the onion is transparent but not browned blend in
    6 Tbs. (90 g) flour.
Cook and stir until the flour just begins to brown. Remove the saucepan
from the heat and add the boiling milk all at once, whisking to blend.
Return to a medium heat and cook, stirring with a wire whip for 5 to 6
minutes until very thick. Season with:
    ½ tsp. (5 g) salt,
    2 grinds of pepper,
    1-2 tsp. paprika, or to taste.
Beat together and then beat into the sauce
    2 eggs.
Cook and stir a moment longer. Fold in
    1½ to 2 cups (375–500 ml) cooked veal, cut in a small dice.
Spread the mixture out into a smooth layer in a buttered 8-inch (20 cm)
square pan. Set aside in the refrigerator to cool and set.

Prepare the Anglaise coating. This coating forms an effective seal that
keeps the croquette crusty on the outside while protecting the creamy
interior from the hot cooking oil. Spread on a plate
    flour.
In a shallow bowl or soup plate beat together the liquid mixture for the
coating:
    1 egg,
    ¼ cup (60 ml) milk,
    1 Tbs. (15 ml) oil,
    ½ tsp. (5 g) salt.
On another plate spread
    fresh bread crumbs made from 5-6 slices of bread, trimmed of
        crusts and reduced in a blender at high speed.

Shape the croquettes. Just before serving time cut the congealed veal
mixture into 4 or 6 sections. Carefully dislodge each section. Croquettes
may be left in these flat squares or rectangles or they may be shaped into
cones, balls, or cylinders.

Coat the croquettes. In the Anglaise fashion, dip the croquette first in
flour, then in the egg-oil mixture, and, finally, in the crumbs patting them
on so that they will adhere well. Make certain all sides and edges are
completely sealed.

Cook the croquettes. Drop one or two at a time into very hot, deep fat
and fry only a few seconds until the bread crumb coating is richly
browned. Remove with a slotted spoon and drain on brown paper. Repeat
until all the croquettes are cooked. Serve at once.

Wine Guide. Serve a Chablis or one of its varietals.

SCALLOPS OF VEAL WITH TARRAGON ████████████████████

Ingredients

scallops of veal	shallot or green onion
salt and pepper	dry white wine
flour	pan sauce† from roasted veal
oil	or brown beef stock*
butter	tarragon

Prepare the veal. Flatten by pounding lightly with a mallet to a thickness of ¼-inch (.5 cm)
　　1 lb. (450 g) veal scallops (sliced from a veal shoulder clod roast).
Season lightly with
　　salt and pepper.
Rub lightly into the scallops on each side
　　flour.
Cook the scallops. Sauté quickly over medium-high heat for 3 to 5 minutes on each side in:
　　1 Tbs. (15 ml) oil,
　　½ Tbs. (8 g) butter.
Remove the scallops to a side dish.
Make the sauce. Pour out all but a small spoonful of cooking fat. Stir in and cook a moment without browning
　　1 shallot or 2 green onions, minced.
Pour in and boil to reduce while scraping the pan to deglaze it:
　　⅓ cup (80 ml) dry white wine,
　　½ cup (125 ml) pan sauce from the braised veal roast, strained, skimmed of all fat; or use beef stock.
When the sauce has reduced and thickened somewhat add
　　½ tsp. dried tarragon, crushed.
Return the scallops to the pan for a quick reheat in the sauce and serve.
Wine Guide. Select a Chablis or one of its varietals.
Variations. (1) Scallops of Veal, Hunter Style. Before sautéing the veal prepare this sauce. Sauté in a small skillet:
　　¼ lb. (120 g) mushrooms, sliced,
　　1 Tbs. (15 g) butter,
　　1 tsp. oil.
When the mushrooms are lightly browned, stir in and cook a moment longer
　　1 large shallot or 2 green onions, minced.
Remove the mushrooms from the pan with a slotted spoon. Add to the skillet
　　2 large tomatoes, peeled, seeded, juiced, chopped.

Cover the skillet and simmer 3-5 minutes to render some of the juices. Remove the lid, raise the heat and cook away most of the moisture from the tomatoes. Add:

> 2 Tbs. (30 ml) dry white wine,
> ½ cup (125 ml) pan sauce from braised roast of veal, strained, skimmed of all fat; or use beef stock.

Boil to reduce by about one-third. Stir into the tomato sauce and set the sauce aside:

> pinch dried tarragon, crushed,
> 2 sprigs parsley, minced,
> the sautéed mushrooms.

Prepare and sauté the scallops as described above. Pour out the cooking fat. Deglaze† the sauté pan with the tomato-mushroom sauce.

(2) Veal Scallops, Parisian Style. Prepare and sauté the scallops as above. Complete the sauce as outlined for Beef Sauté, Parisian Style.*

Supplement for Calf's Liver

The recipes below demonstrate how easily fresh or previously cooked calf's liver substitutes for veal scallops or other veal variations.

SAUTÉED CALF'S LIVER ▮▮▮▮▮▮▮▮▮▮▮▮▮▮▮▮▮▮▮▮▮▮

Prepare the meat. Season slices of calf's liver lightly with
> salt and pepper.

Dip them in flour, shaking off any excess.

Cook the liver. Sauté the slices quickly (as described above for veal scallops) for 2 to 3 minutes on a side in
> 1½ Tbs. each (45 g total) butter and oil.

Serve at once. Spread with a composed butter* or proceed to the pan deglazing sauce described for Scallops of Veal* substituting for the white wine and pan sauce
> ½ cup (125 ml) beef stock.

Instead of tarragon add
> 2 sprigs parsley, chopped.

Spoon the sauce over the liver and serve.

Wine Guide. Select a Rosé wine.

Variation. Calf's Liver, Hunter Style. Follow the procedure for Veal Scallops, Hunter Style* but, again, omit the tarragon and use about ½ cup (125 ml) beef stock instead of pan sauce from the roast.

Note. Chicken livers may also be prepared in this manner.

SERVING SUGGESTIONS FOR PREVIOUSLY COOKED LIVER

(1) *Liver croquettes.* Make the same sauce described for Veal Croquettes* but substitute for the paprika
> pinch of nutmeg.

Also add to the sauce
    2 sprigs parsley, chopped.
Fold into the sauce:
    1 cup (250 ml) cooked calf's liver, diced,
    ½ cup (125 ml) stale bread, cut in a small dice.
Allow the mixture to set. Cut into serving size pieces. Shape as desired. Coat by the Anglaise method* and fry in deep fat. Refer to the veal recipe for details. Garnish with lemon wedges.

(2) *Liver in tomato sauce.* Cooked liver may be diced and very gently reheated in tomato sauce.* This is especially good with the Mediterranean seasonings given in the variation. Serve with pasta.

Breast of Veal

Order a 6 lb. (3 kg) veal breast boned. The remaining preparation you may do yourself according to the directions given in the recipe below. The bones can be used in making a stock to braise the veal breast and to make the stew that follows. Any remaining stock may be used in a soup or as the basis for sauce Espagnole.*

The Stuffed Breast of Veal to follow is delightfully fragrant and colorful. Remaining meat may be used in a stew† or in crêpes which utilize both the meat and the filling. The ground veal loaf at the end of this section presents an unusual and delicious flavor combination. Ground veal can also be used to make veal burgers in the same way as lamburgers* are made.

STUFFED BREAST OF VEAL ▐▬▬▬▬▬▬▬▬▬▬▬▬▬▬▬▬▪

Ingredients

stock made from veal bones	butter
carrots	shallots or green onions
onion	dry white wine
celery	Boston lettuce
parsley	egg
thyme	cottage cheese, uncreamed
bay leaf	nutmeg
salt and pepper	breast of veal, boned
French or sourdough bread	oil

Preheat the oven 450 F (210 C).

Make the brown veal stock. This step is best accomplished a day in advance. Brown together in an open roasting pan for 30 to 40 minutes:
    the bones removed from a breast of veal,
    2 carrots, sliced,
    1 onion, sliced.
Following the procedure described for brown beef stock* place the browned veal bones and vegetables in a kettle and cover them with cold

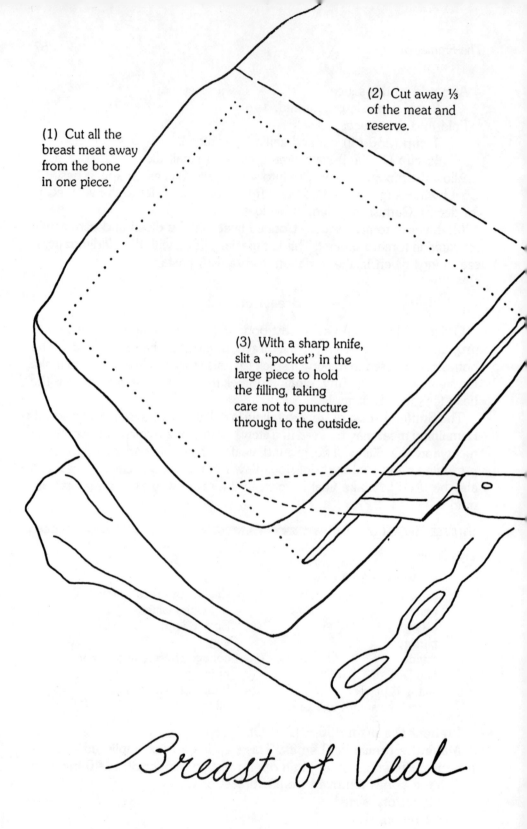

(1) Cut all the breast meat away from the bone in one piece.

(2) Cut away ⅓ of the meat and reserve.

(3) With a sharp knife, slit a "pocket" in the large piece to hold the filling, taking care not to puncture through to the outside.

Breast of Veal

water. Pour out the fat from the roasting pan and deglaze† it. Bring the contents of the kettle to simmer, removing the scum as it rises. Season the stock with

> ½ tsp. (5 g) salt.

Add a bouquet of herbs:

> 1 stalk celery,
> 4 sprigs parsley,
> ⅓ domestic bay leaf.

Simmer the stock for 3–4 hours. Skim and discard the fat from the surface and use this stock as the braising liquid for the breast of veal.

Preheat the oven 200 F (80 C).

Prepare the stuffing. Dry out in the low-heated oven

> 2 slices French or sourdough bread, trimmed of crusts.

Cut the bread in a small dice. Cook together over low heat in a small skillet:

> 3 Tbs. (45 g) butter,
> 2 shallots or green onions, minced.

After 5 minutes add and cook 3-5 minutes longer

> 1 Tbs. (15 ml) dry white wine.

Combine the bread, butter, and shallots or onions in a bowl. Thoroughly wash and separate the leaves of

> 1 head of Boston lettuce.

Drop the leaves in a kettle of boiling water for 3-5 minutes until wilted. Drain the lettuce; squeeze it dry and chop it finely. Add the lettuce to the bowl and also blend in:

> 1 egg,
> ½ cup (125 ml) uncreamed cottage cheese,
> 3 sprigs parsley, chopped,
> pinch thyme,
> pinch nutmeg,
> salt and pepper, lightly sprinkled.

Prepare the boned breast of veal for stuffing. Following the illustration, remove a section weighing approximately 1 lb. (450 g) to be frozen and used later for veal loaf. Cut a pocket in the part of the breast to be stuffed. Proceed carefully with a sharp knife to make an incision along one lengthwise edge. Continue cutting parallel to the underside of the roast until a pocket is made that extends to within an inch (2 cm) of the other three edges. Take care not to puncture the meat to the outside.

Stuff the veal breast. Distribute the prepared stuffing evenly in the pocket. Tie the roast in 2 or 3 places to hold the stuffing in the pocket.

Preheat the oven 350 F (160 C).

Brown the roast. Over medium-high heat in a heavy casserole, brown both sides of the stuffed veal breast in:

> 2 Tbs. (30 ml) oil,
> 1 Tbs. (15 g) butter.

Remove the roast from the casserole. Stir into the fat and brown lightly:

 1 small carrot, sliced,
 1 small onion, sliced.

Remove any excess fat from the casserole. Season the roast lightly with
 salt and pepper.

Return the roast to the casserole, placing it over the vegetables. Pour in:

 2 cups (500 ml) brown veal stock, previously prepared,
 ½ cup (125 ml) dry white wine.

Add a bouquet of herbs:

 1 stalk celery,
 3 sprigs parsley,
 pinch thyme,
 ¼ domestic bay leaf.

Lay a piece of buttered brown paper over the meat and bring the
contents to simmering on top of the stove. Place the casserole in the
preheated oven and braise for about 2 hours (until tender), basting well
every half-hour.

Complete the sauce. Serve the roast with the pan sauce skimmed of
fat, with the cooking vegetables mashed into the braising liquid.

Wine Guide. Select a dry white Chablis or one of its varietals.

VEAL STEW WITH MUSHROOMS AND CREAM

Ingredients

mushrooms	bay leaf
oil	basil
onion	parsley
veal stock and/or pan sauce†	butter
dry white wine	flour
tomato, optional	veal, previously roasted
garlic, optional	cream

Prepare the vegetables. Sauté in a heavy casserole until lightly
browned:

 6 large mushrooms, sliced,
 2 Tbs. (30 ml) oil.

Remove the mushrooms with a slotted spoon. Set them aside until later.
Add:

 1 medium onion, sliced,
 more oil, if necessary.

Brown the onions lightly and remove them to a side dish with a slotted
spoon. Pour out all but 1 Tbs. (15 ml) fat from the pan. Stir in and brown
lightly

 1 Tbs. (15 g) flour.

Add the liquid. Pour into the casserole:

¾ cup (180 ml) veal stock or use the strained, skimmed pan sauce from the preceding roast and water, if necessary,

¼ cup (60 ml) dry white wine.

Bring to boiling, and add:

the browned mushrooms,

the sautéed onions,

1 tomato, peeled, seeded, chopped, optional,

1 clove garlic, crushed, peeled, optional,

pinch basil if including tomato and garlic or, otherwise,

pinch thyme,

⅓ domestic bay leaf,

2 sprigs parsley.

Cook the sauce. Cover the casserole and simmer on low heat for 20 minutes to blend the flavors.

Final steps. Add and gently reheat:

the cooked veal left from the preceding roast, stuffing removed, cut in pieces,

⅓ cup (80 ml) cream.

Serve with rice or noodles.

Wine Guide. Select a Chablis or Claret or one of their varietals.

Variations. (1) To make this stew from uncooked veal, dry the pieces, roll them in flour, brown in butter and oil, and add the meat at the beginning of the simmering time. Cook with stock and seasonings for about 1 hour in a preheated 350 F (160 C) oven.

(2) Filling for crêpes. Grind the cooked veal and stuffing together. Make a béchamel sauce,* doubling the amounts given. Mix half of the sauce with the ground meat and filling and reserve half to pour over the completed dish. Spread the filling mixture between crêpes arranged in a stack (see Index; crêpes, final presentation). Cover the stack of crêpes with the reserved béchamel sauce. Dot the top with butter and reheat 30 minutes before serving in the upper level of a preheated 375 F (170 C) oven.

MEDITERRANEAN VEAL LOAF ▰▰▰▰▰▰▰▰▰▰▰▰▰▰▰

Ingredients

ground veal	salt and pepper
bread	tuna
milk or stock	anchovies
butter	ripe olives
onion	bacon
garlic	lemon slices
parsley	
basil	

Preheat the oven 350 F (160 C).

Prepare the meat. Defrost and grind while still slightly crystalline
   approximately 2 cups (500 ml) ground veal, weighing about 1 lb.
      (450 g).

Place the ground veal in a bowl.

Soak together:
   2 slices bread, trimmed of crusts,
   ½ cup (125 ml) milk or stock.

In a small skillet sauté together:
   3 Tbs. (45 g) butter,
   ½ medium onion, diced,
   1 clove garlic, crushed, peeled.

Add the butter and onions to the meat. Squeeze the bread dry and add
the dough-like mass to the bowl along with:
   3 sprigs parsley, minced,
   pinch basil,
   few grinds pepper,
   salt, very lightly.

Beat with a wooden spoon to blend well.

Assemble the loaf. Pack half of the meat mixture into a loaf pan.
Arrange over it:
   ½ cup (125 ml) canned tuna, drained, flaked,
   4-6 anchovies,
   8-10 whole, pitted olives.

Pack the remaining half of the meat mixture over the tuna, anchovies,
and olives. Lay over the top of the loaf
   3 strips bacon, simmered 10 minutes in
   1 qt. (1 l) water, drained, rinsed, dried.

Bake for 1 hour in the preheated oven. Pour off the fat. Unmold the loaf
and serve with a garnish of
   lemon slices.

Wine Guide. Select a Chablis, Claret, one of their varietals, or a
Beaujolais.

Veal Hind Shank

Hind shank is the traditional and preferred cut to use for the stew below.
If it is unavailable, select some other cut suitable for stewing such as neck
bones, short ribs, or shoulder chops.

ITALIAN VEAL STEW WITH ORANGE (OSSOBUCO) ████████████████

Ingredients

| hind shank of veal | flour | onions |
| salt and pepper | oil | carrot |

celery	thyme	chicken stock*
garlic	marjoram	brown beef stock*
tomatoes	oregano	dry white wine
tomato paste	rosemary	orange
parsley	bay leaf	lemon

Preheat the oven 325 F (150 C).

Prepare the meat. Order

> hind shank of veal cut into 6 slices, each about 2½ inches (6 cm)
> thick.

Season the slices of meat with

> salt and pepper.

Dust them very lightly with

> flour.

Brown the slices of veal shank in a heavy casserole over medium-high heat, 2 or 3 pieces at a time in

> 2 Tbs. (30 ml) hot oil, adding more if necessary.

Remove the meat to a side dish as it is browned.

Add the seasonings:

> 2 small onions, thinly sliced,
> 1 carrot, thinly sliced,
> 1 stalk celery, thinly sliced.

Cook until the onion is transparent. Stir in and simmer gently for 2-3 minutes

> 1 large clove garlic, crushed, peeled.

Add:

> 2 tomatoes, peeled, seeded, juiced, chopped,
> 1 tsp. tomato paste,
> 3 sprigs parsley, chopped,
> pinch each of thyme, marjoram, oregano, rosemary,
> ⅓ domestic bay leaf,
> salt and pepper lightly to taste.

Simmer a few minutes and then add:

> ½ cup (125 ml) chicken stock,
> ½ cup (125 ml) beef stock,
> ⅔ cup (160 ml) dry white wine,
> zest† of 1 orange and 1 lemon: cut the colored part from the rinds
> and simmer it 10 minutes, drain, cut in thin julienne† strips.

Cook the stew. Return the browned veal to the casserole and bring the contents to simmering. Cover and set in a preheated oven. Cook for 2 hours or until the meat is tender.

Serve. Accompany the stew with risotto.* Broccoli with lemon butter and bacon* makes an excellent first course for this dish.

Wine Guide. Select a white Chablis or one of its varietals.

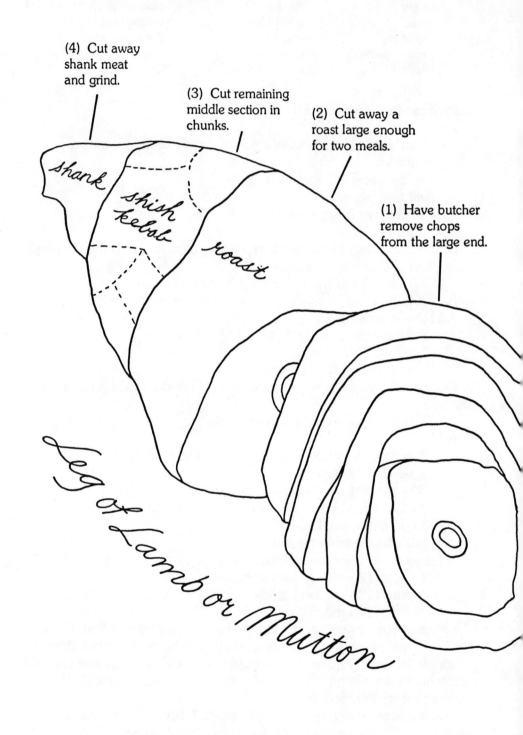

(4) Cut away shank meat and grind.

(3) Cut remaining middle section in chunks.

(2) Cut away a roast large enough for two meals.

(1) Have butcher remove chops from the large end.

shank

shish kebob

roast

Leg of Lamb or Mutton

MEDITERRANEAN SOUP ███

Ingredients

navy or Great Northern beans	remaining veal stew
zucchini	Swiss cheese
spaghetti	hard rolls

Convert the veal stew. Any remaining stew may be changed slightly to make a main dish soup. Set a sieve over a large bowl. Pour the stew into the sieve to strain out the gravy from the meat and vegetables. Rinse the meat to remove any pieces of orange and lemon rind which may cling to it. Cut up the meat and add it to the stew gravy. The soup will retain a hint of the citrus flavor but the rind and stew vegetables should be discarded. Add water to thin the gravy and add new vegetables:

⅓ to ½ cup (80–125 ml) navy or Great Northern beans, previously soaked and simmered until almost tender,

1-2 zucchini, sliced.

Cook the soup. Simmer ½ hour and add

⅓ cup (80 ml) broken spaghetti.

Simmer until the pasta is cooked al dente.†

Serve. Accompany with:

grated Swiss cheese,

dried round slices of French rolls.

Wine Guide. Choose a Chablis or Claret or one of their varietals.

Leg of Lamb or Mutton

A leg as large as the one described in this section would more properly be termed a leg of mutton, but the ideas may be applied to smaller pieces as well. A leg of lamb may also be divided before cooking, but it will not provide as many meals as a leg of mutton. Adjustments may easily be made according to size.

The butcher should cut the chops off the end and you may ask him to section the remainder for you. It is often more advisable, however, to assume that task yourself. You can then look the piece over carefully and better judge exactly where the cuts should be made to allow adequate portions for each serving, for each purpose.

Butchering the leg is not difficult. All you need is a short, stout saw from the tool chest. Thoroughly wash and scald it. With a sharp knife, cut through the meat to the bone at the determined place and saw until the bone is severed. Reserve all bones for the stew.

The large 9 lb. (4 kg) leg of mutton used here had four generous chops cut from the large loin end. The shank was removed from the other end. About one-third of the middle section was removed and cut into pieces for use in shish kabob. The remaining, largest section was roasted. Two recipes are provided for utilizing previously cooked lamb or mutton. Variations and serving suggestions following some of the lamb recipes offer alternatives treated in other sections.

SAUTÉED LAMB CHOPS

Ingredients

lamb chops	shallot or green onions
oil	dry white wine
butter	parsley
salt and pepper	

Sauté the chops. Sautéing lamb chops over a hot flame is a means of pan broiling and should not be confused with "frying." The chops are succulent because their juices are sealed at once, but enough residue remains in the pan to produce a few delicious spoonfuls of sauce. The particular advantage of this method is that it allows you to carefully control the cooking process and degree of doneness. In 1 or 2 skillets, heat enough butter and oil to cover the bottom of the pan, about:

1 Tbs. (15 ml) oil,
½ Tbs. (8 g) butter.

As the mixture heats you may find it necessary to pour out some of the fat before adding the chops. Keep only enough to prevent the meat from sticking to the pan. Heat over medium-high heat until the butter foams and begins to subside. Add in one layer

4–6 large loin lamb chops.

Cook 3 to 5 minutes on each side depending on the thickness of the chops.

Control the degree of doneness. Pan sautéed meat is medium-rare the moment it becomes resistant to the touch of a finger (until that point it will feel soft when pressed with the forefinger). Doneness may be double-checked, however, by making a tiny incision in the chop (or steak). If it is not yet done it may be returned to the pan without harm for additional cooking.

Season the chops. When the chops are done remove them to a hot platter and season lightly with

salt and pepper.

Make the pan deglazing sauce. Pour out the sauté fat. Stir into the small amount of fat which remains in the pan

1 large shallot or 2 green onions, minced.

Cook-stir a moment and then pour in to deglaze the pan

⅓ cup (80 ml) dry white wine.

Raise the heat and scrape the pan to incorporate the juices. Boil down rapidly to reduce to half. Stir in:

2 sprigs parsley, minced,
½ Tbs. (8 g) butter, optional.

Serve. Spread the sauce over the chops and serve at once. They may be accompanied with braised onions,* sautéed potatoes, and sautéed mushrooms.*

Wine Guide. Select a Chablis, a Claret, or a Beaujolais, or for mutton, a Burgundy.

Note. The methods of broiling and pan sautéing are interchangeable for lamb chops and beef steaks. When beef steaks are pan sautéed, as above, the pan sauce is usually made with a red wine instead of white. The alternate method for lamb chops usually requires broiling 3 to 5 minutes on a side, depending on thickness.

Roast Leg of Lamb ▰▰▰▰▰▰▰▰▰▰▰▰▰▰▰▰

Ingredients

> leg of lamb
> oil
> salt and pepper
> carrot
> onion
> brown beef stock*

Preheat the oven 450 F (210 C).

Prepare the meat for roasting. Brush the exterior of a
> 4-5 lb. (2–2.5 kg) leg of lamb with
> cooking oil.

Season it lightly with
> salt and pepper.

Set it in a roasting pan on a bed of vegetables:
> 1 large carrot, sliced,
> 1 medium onion, sliced.

Roast the meat. Place the pan on a middle-low rack in the preheated oven to sear for 15 minutes. Reduce the heat to 350 F (160 C) and continue to roast until medium-rare. Count 12 to 15 minutes per pound. Remove the leg of lamb onto a hot platter and allow it to rest 20 minutes before carving.

Prepare the pan deglazing sauce. Pour out the fat from the roasting pan. Pour in and bring quickly to boiling
> 1 cup (250 ml) beef stock.

Scrape the pan to incorporate all the browned drippings. Cook the sauce down to concentrate its flavor.

Serve. Slice the roast and strain a spoonful of sauce over each serving. Serve at once on hot plates. Reserve the remaining pan sauce for other recipes in this section.

Wine Guide. Serve roast lamb with a Claret, roast mutton with a Burgundy.

Variation. See note 2 after Pork Roast Boulangère.*

LAMB STEW WITH SPRING VEGETABLES ▬▬▬▬▬▬▬▬▬▬▬▬▬

Ingredients

previously roasted lamb	rosemary
oil	bay leaf
bones	potatoes
sugar	turnips
flour	carrots
pan sauce† and water	onions
tomato paste	green beans, previously
garlic	cooked
thyme	peas, previously cooked

Preheat the oven 350 F (160 C).

Prepare the meat. Cut into large chunks and dry well on paper towels
    the cold meat remaining from the previously roasted leg of lamb.
Heat in a heavy skillet
    2 Tbs. (30 ml) oil.
Brown in the hot oil
    the bones from the leg of lamb from the previously roasted piece
        and those saved from butchering the other sections of the leg.
Remove the bones when they have browned well on all sides. Add the
meat to the hot oil and sprinkle with
    ¼ tsp. sugar (to hasten the browning).
As soon as the meat has a light brown color remove it from the skillet
and set it aside until later.

Prepare the sauce. Pour out all but a spoonful of fat from the skillet and
make a rich brown roux† by adding to the skillet and cooking
    1½ Tbs. (20 g) flour.
When the roux is well browned pour in
    the pan sauce remaining from the preceding roast of lamb,
        skimmed off fat and mixed with enough water to make 1½ cups
        (375 ml) liquid in all.
Cook, scraping the sides and bottom of the pan to blend in the browned
pieces. Add and simmer a little to combine the flavors:
    1 Tbs. tomato paste,
    1 clove garlic, crushed, peeled,
    pinch each of thyme, rosemary,
    ¼ domestic bay leaf.
Pour the sauce over the bones in the casserole.

Prepare the vegetables. Parboil† for 3 minutes
    2 turnips, peeled, quartered.
Add the turnips to the casserole and also add:
    6-8 small onions, peeled,
    2 potatoes, peeled, quartered,
    3-4 carrots, peeled, quartered.

Cook the casserole. Cover and bake for about 1 hour in the preheated oven.

Complete the dish. Remove the casserole from the oven. Take the bones out of the casserole and fold in
> the prepared lamb that was set aside.

Arrange over the top
> ⅓ cup (80 ml) each, precooked green beans and peas, defrosted, if frozen.

Baste the vegetables with some of the sauce. Cover and return the casserole to the oven for 15 minutes longer until the green vegetables and meat are heated through and the other vegetables are tender.

Serve. Accompany the stew with a green salad and French bread to take up the sauce.

Wine Guide. Select a Chablis, a Claret, or one of their varietals.

Note. Just as in the preceding beef and veal stews, this lamb stew recipe exploits the technique of using roasted meat in a stew.† If you wish to convert this recipe to the original, brown uncooked lamb with the bones and simmer them with seasonings (a bouquet of herbs,† browned onion and carrot, tomato paste, and garlic) in beef stock to cover for 1 hour before adding the first vegetables. Then, proceed as described to the end of the recipe.

Variations. Previously cooked lamb may also be utilized in Cassoulet* or Spanish Pork and Rice.*

MOUSSAKA ██████████████████████████

Ingredients

tomato sauce*	flour
roasted lamb	pan sauce† and water
eggplant	tomato paste
salt and pepper	thyme
mushrooms	rosemary
oil	egg
onion	sour cream or yogurt
garlic	dill

This dish is a delectable alternative to the preceding stew.

Make in advance
> tomato sauce.

Only about half of the recipe is required for moussaka; the remainder may be used with Lamb Shish Kebab, below.

Prepare the meat. Grind
> cooked lamb remaining from the previous roast, up to 1½ cups (375 ml).

Prepare the vegetables. Pull off the green tops from
> 2 small eggplants, weighing 2 lbs. (2 kg) total.

Cut them in half lengthwise. Slice 4-6 deep gashes from top to bottom into the cut surface, stopping ¼-inch (.5 cm) from the skin. Then, to draw out excess moisture, sprinkle over the cut surfaces

    1 tsp. (5 g) salt.

Let them stand for 30 minutes. Meanwhile, sauté in a heavy skillet:

    6 medium mushrooms, sliced,

    2 Tbs. (30 ml) oil.

When the mushrooms are lightly browned, remove them with a slotted spoon and set aside in a large bowl. Add to the skillet with more oil, if necessary:

    1 medium onion, sliced,

    1 clove garlic, crushed, peeled, chopped.

Cook over medium heat until very lightly browned. Remove the onions and garlic with a slotted spoon and add them to the bowl with the mushrooms. After half-an-hour, squeeze the rendered water from the salted eggplant and dry it as much as possible on paper towels. Scoop out the pulp and chop it in a large dice. Add more oil to the skillet if required and brown the diced eggplant lightly. Then add it to the bowl along with the other vegetables.

Preheat the oven 350 F (160 C).

Make a brown sauce. In the skillet used for the vegetables make a roux by browning together:

    1½ Tbs. (20 ml) oil,

    1½ Tbs. (20 g) flour.

When the roux is a nut brown color, add all at once, stirring to smooth and blend

    the pan sauce left from the roasted leg of lamb, skimmed of all fat,
        about ½–¾ cup and

    enough water to make 1 cup (250 ml)
        liquid altogether.

When the sauce is thick and smooth, blend in:

    1 Tbs. tomato paste,

    1 pinch each of thyme and rosemary.

Simmer a moment to blend the flavors.

Complete the filling. Scrape this sauce into the eggplant mixture and blend well. Taste carefully and season as required with

    salt and pepper.

Beat in

    1 egg.

Assemble the dish. In a heavy casserole, alternate layers of the eggplant mixture with layers of ground lamb, ending with a layer of eggplant on top. Pour the tomato sauce over the top. Cover the casserole and bake in the preheated oven for 1¼ hours.

Serve. Give the moussaka a characteristic Rumanian touch by garnishing it just before serving with

⅓ cup (80 ml) sour cream or yogurt and

a sprinkle of dill.

Wine Guide. Select a Chablis, a Claret, one of their varietals, or a Beaujolais.

LAMB SHISH KEBAB

Ingredients

lemon juice	lamb (uncooked)
oil	mushrooms
salt and pepper	bacon
parsley	
thyme	
bay leaf	
garlic	

Marinate the lamb. As illustrated, cut into pieces

1–1¼ lb (450–560 g) lamb cut in 1½-inch cubes (3.5 cm cubed).

Make a lemon juice vinaigrette. Combine in a jar:

2 Tbs. (30 ml) freshly squeezed lemon juice,

2 Tbs. (30 ml) oil,

½ tsp. salt,

3 grinds of pepper,

3 sprigs parsley, crushed,

pinch thyme,

½ domestic bay leaf, crumbled,

1 clove garlic, crushed, peeled.

Shake the jar to blend the vinaigrette and pour it over the lamb. Marinate the pieces of meat, turning occasionally, for 1 to 1½ hours.

Prepare for cooking. Thread on long skewers:

the pieces of marinated lamb,

whole mushrooms,

strips of bacon.

Broil. Baste with the marinade and turn every minute or two. Cook 5 to 7 minutes until the meat is browned.

Serve. Unskewer the shish kebab over a bed of risotto* and accompany with tomato sauce,* if desired.

Wine Guide. Select a Chablis, Claret, one of their varietals, or a Beaujolais.

Note. This marinade also works well with pork to enhance the flavor of roasts and chops prior to cooking.

LAMBURGERS ██

Ingredients

ground, uncooked lamb	thyme
cooked rice	tomato
salt and pepper	egg
butter	flour
onion	oil
garlic	brown beef stock*
parsley	

Prepare the meat mixture. The patties require time in the refrigerator to chill so they must be prepared and shaped several hours in advance or the night before. Grind
 lamb from the shank portion of the leg, about 1½ cups (375 ml) when ground, grinding the last few pieces with
 ½ cup (125 ml) cooked rice.
Put the ground lamb and rice in a bowl and season lightly with
 salt and pepper.
In a small skillet melt
 1 Tbs. (15 g) butter.
Add and cook gently until transparent
 ½ small onion, finely chopped.
Stir in and cook a moment longer
 ½ clove garlic, minced.
Add:
 2 sprigs parsley, minced,
 pinch thyme,
 1 tomato, peeled, seeded, juiced, chopped.
Cover and cook slowly for 3–4 minutes to render the juices. Remove the lid, raise the heat, and cook-stir until as much moisture as possible has been evaporated. Add this thickened tomato sauce to the ground lamb and rice in the bowl. Beat in
 1 egg.
Beat all the ingredients together with a wooden spoon to blend well.
 Shape into 4 patties. The mixture will be soft and difficult to shape, but it will set while chilling. Arrange the patties around the edge of a plate, leaving a space in the center. Lay a piece of waxed paper over them and chill in the refrigerator.
 Cook the lamburgers. About half an hour before serving, sift into the center of the plate of patties
 ½ cup (125 ml) flour.
Dredge each lamburger in flour, coating sides and edges, and gently shake off the excess. Heat in a heavy skillet over medium-high heat until the butter foams and nearly subsides:
 1½ Tbs. (20 g) butter,
 1 Tbs. (15 ml) oil.

Add the patties and brown them 3 minutes on each side. Pour out most of the fat leaving only a spoonful. Turn the heat to low; cover the skillet and cook slowly 15 minutes longer. Turn the lamburgers once during this time. Remove them to a platter and pour out all the fat from the skillet.

Make the sauce. Pour into the skillet

⅓ cup (80 ml) beef stock.

Cook, scraping the pan while boiling the stock down rapidly to deglaze†️ the pan. Stir in

1 tsp. (5 g) butter, optional.

Serve. Spread a spoonful of sauce over each of the lamb patties and serve at once.

Wine Guide. Select a Chablis, Claret, one of their varietals, or a Beaujolais.

Notes. (1) For more than four patties, the amount of meat may be extended by adding lean, ground pork or pork sausage.

(2) Ground veal may be substituted for lamb in this recipe.

SERVING SUGGESTIONS

(1) *Lamb shoulder roast.* A boned shoulder of lamb may be stuffed very much like Stuffed Breast of Veal.* For the stuffing make these substitutions:

1 large clove of garlic (for the shallots),

spinach (for the lettuce),

sausage (for the cottage cheese).

Fill the pockets where the bones were removed with the stuffing, roll the roast lengthwise, and tie it securely. Following the general procedure for browning given for stuffed breast of veal, brown the tied roast, then brown the bones taken from the shoulder. Add the wine and seasonings and

2 cups (500 ml) brown beef stock.*

Place the bones in the casserole around the roast and braise.†️

(2) *Stuffed leg of lamb.* With a boning knife (short, stout, sharp knife), split open a leg of lamb and remove the bone. Fill with the stuffing described above; roll, tie, and braise.†️

Pork Shoulder Roast

The next two sections demonstrate two very different methods for preparing a pork roast. In this section, the meat is simply roasted in an open pan on a bed of potatoes. The alternate plan, taken up in the next section, is the closed casserole roasting method. This technique works beautifully with pork (and also with chicken).

Pork, no matter how it is prepared, is always cooked well-done and tends toward dryness. Therefore, it is the most difficult meat to reuse after it has been cooked. In the Spanish rice and cassoulet recipes to follow, rice and beans are used to insulate the meat. Consequently, the pork is just heated through by the time the other ingredients have completed cooking. Alternatively, cooked pork may be diced, used in a composed salad, cooked as croquettes,* or ground and used in spreads.

PORK ROAST BOULANGÈRE ████████████████████████████████████

Ingredients

pork shoulder roast	onion
salt and pepper	parsley
potatoes	butter

Preheat the oven 425 F (200 C).

Brown the roast. Place in a large roasting pan
    4-5 lb. (2–2.5 kg) shoulder (or loin) roast of pork.
Season it lightly with
    salt and pepper.
Set the pan in the middle of a hot preheated oven for 1 hour. Baste the roast with the rendered pork fat and turn it often. Remove the meat to a plate.

Make a pan deglazing sauce. Pour the fat from the roasting pan and pour in
    1 cup (250 ml) water.
Bring the water to boiling and scrape up the coagulated juices. Continue boiling to reduce by about one-third. Season the pan sauce with
    salt and pepper.
Pour off this sauce from the roasting pan and reserve it until later.

Arrange the vegetables. Prepare
    8 small potatoes, peeled and sliced.
Spread half the potatoes in a layer in the roasting pan. Cover with:
    1 onion, chopped,
    2 sprigs parsley, chopped,
    salt and pepper, lightly sprinkled.
Make another layer with the remaining potatoes. Add over the top:
    salt and pepper,
    2 Tbs. (30 g) butter, broken in pieces.
Return the pork roast to the pan, placing it on the potatoes. Pour into the pan
    hot water to nearly cover the potatoes.
Bring to a boil on the top of the stove.

Reduce the oven setting to 400 F (185 C).

Final roasting. Return the pan to the oven to cook for 1½ hours longer. The water will have nearly cooked away and the potatoes will be brown on top.

Serve. Transfer the potatoes to a platter. Arrange the meat, carved in slices, over the top. Add any remaining juices from the pan to the reserved

deglazing sauce. Reheat the pan sauce and swirl in
> ½ to 1 Tbs. (8-15 g) butter, optional.

Ladle a spoonful or two of the sauce over each slice of meat as it is served.

Wine Guide. Select a Rhine wine or one of its varietals or a Chablis.

Notes. (1) Make a potato soup from any potatoes that remain by adding a little stock or water and mashing in the potatoes with a fork. Simmer awhile to blend the flavors. Just before serving, stir in 1-2 Tbs. (15-30 ml) cream.

(2) A leg of lamb may also be prepared this way. Brush it with cooking oil before the initial searing. When it is returned to the oven to finish roasting over the potatoes, cook it for only 1 hour.

SPANISH PORK AND RICE

Ingredients

bacon	pan sauce† from roasted pork
butter	chicken stock*
rice	tomato paste
salt	thyme
onion	bay leaf
garlic	saffron
tomatoes	roasted pork
dry white wine	Swiss cheese

Initial steps. Blanch† the bacon by simmering for 10 minutes:
> 3 slices of bacon in
> 1 qt. (1 l) water.

Drain the bacon, rinse it in cold water and dry in paper towels. Cut each strip of bacon into about 8 crosscut pieces. In a small skillet melt
> 1 Tbs. (15 g) butter.

Add the bacon and brown lightly. Add
> ¾ cup (180 ml) rice.

Cook and stir over medium heat until the rice turns a chalky white color. Scrape the rice and bacon into a side bowl and sprinkle very lightly with
> salt.

Prepare the tomato sauce. In the same skillet melt again
> 1 Tbs. (15 g) butter
and brown lightly in it
> 1 small onion, sliced.

Stir in and cook a minute longer
> 1 clove garlic, crushed, peeled.

Add to the skillet, cover, and cook over medium-low heat for 5 to 8 minutes to render the juices of
> 2 tomatoes, peeled, seeded, chopped.

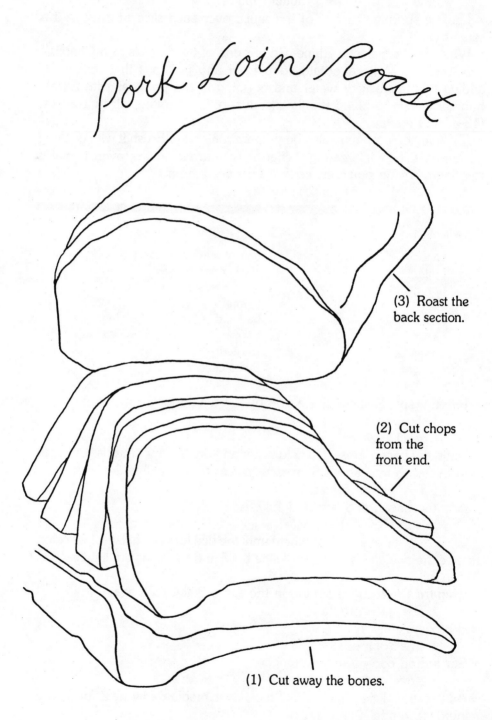

Pork Loin Roast

(3) Roast the back section.

(2) Cut chops from the front end.

(1) Cut away the bones.

Pour into a 1 pt. (500 ml) measuring cup:
> ¼ cup (60 ml) dry white wine,
> any deglazed pan juices saved from the roast, skimmed of all fat.

Place a strainer over the measuring cup. Empty the tomato-onion mixture into the strainer. Let the vegetable juices drain into the measuring cup containing the white wine and pan sauce. Then add
> enough chicken stock to make 1½ cups (375 ml) liquid (in which to cook the rice).

Return the tomato-onion mixture and the liquids to the skillet. Heat to simmering and season this tomato sauce with:
> 1 tsp. tomato paste,
> pinch thyme,
> pinch salt,
> ¼ domestic bay leaf,
> pinch saffron.

Assemble the casserole. Cut up and place in a lightly buttered 1½ qt. (1.5 l) casserole
> the remaining meat from a roasted pork shoulder.

Bring the tomato sauce to a slow boil. Blend in the rice and bacon; bring again to boiling. Pour the tomato sauce and rice into the casserole with the meat. Cover and bake in the middle of the preheated oven for 20–25 minutes.

Final garnish. Upon removing the casserole from the oven, sprinkle over the top and toss with a fork to blend
> ½ cup (125 ml) grated Swiss cheese.

Wine Guide. Select a Chablis, Claret, one of their varietals, or a Beaujolais.

Note. Beef or lamb may be substituted for pork, but beef stock should be used in the place of chicken stock and the meat should be quickly browned before adding it to the casserole.

Pork Loin Roast

For the following recipes, order a large loin roast of pork weighing about 6½ lbs. (3 kg). Have it boned and a few chops removed from the end.

The cuts in this section will be marinated, not to tenderize them, but to enhance the flavor of the pork. A dry salt marinade is used with the roast and a wine and oil combination for the ribs. The lemon juice vinaigrette* used for Lamb Shish Kebab is also good for pork and it may be substituted in any of these recipes.

Pork chops, marinated or not, respond very well to closed pan roasting methods. Pork and chicken are among the few meats successfully cooked in this manner. Closed pan roasting differs from braising† in that no liquid is added to the casserole for the period of slow cooking. However, pork roasts may be braised as well; directions are noted at the end of the first recipe in this section. Browned pork roast, chops, or ribs may also be braised with sauerkraut as in Choucroute Garni.*

Boneless Roast of Pork

Ingredients

salt and pepper	carrot
bay leaf	onion
allspice	celery
cloves	parsley
thyme	stock, water, or dry white wine
boneless roast of pork	

Marinate the meat. For every 2 pounds (1 kg) of meat combine:
    ½ tsp. salt,
    ½ domestic bay leaf, crushed,
    1 pinch each of pepper, allspice, cloves, thyme.
Rub the mixture into the
    boneless pork roast.
Marinate for several hours.
Preheat the oven 425 F (200 C).
Cook the roast. Scrape off the marinade and dry the meat well. Place the roast, fat side up, in a heavy casserole on a bed of vegetables:
    1 carrot, sliced,
    1 onion, sliced.
Brown in a hot, preheated oven for 25-30 minutes.
Reduce the heat to 325 F (150 C).
Add a bouquet of herbs to the casserole:
    1 celery stalk,
    4 sprigs parsley,
    1/2 domestic bay leaf,
    pinch thyme.
Cover the casserole and cook until the meat tests well-done—about 1–1½ hours for a 3 lb. (1.5 kg) roast. When it is done remove the roast from the casserole.
Finish the sauce. Pour in
    1 cup (250 ml) stock, water, or dry white wine.
Mash in the vegetables and boil rapidly to reduce the sauce to ¾ cup (180 ml). Apportion the pan sauce sparingly; the remainder will be added to the cassoulet.
Wine Guide. Select a white wine from the chart.
Notes. (1) A pork roast may also be braised. Follow the initial preparation and browning procedure outlined for covered roasting above. When the heat is reduced and the herbs added to the casserole, pour in 1 cup

(250 ml) stock or water. Cover and cook about 1½ hours.

(2) To braise a boneless roast of beef, such as a whole filet, follow the alternate procedure explained in Note 1, above. Substitute dry white wine for the stock. Lay a piece of buttered brown paper over the meat. Check for doneness (to medium-rare) in 40-45 minutes. A boneless beef roast may also be marinated before cooking. Use the proportions given for Pork Ribs in Red Wine Marinade,* and make the following substitutions: dry white wine for the red wine; shallots or green onions for the garlic; basil for the fennel. The marinade may constitute part of the braising liquid.

CASSOULET (FRENCH BAKED BEANS)

Ingredients

navy or Great Northern beans	thyme
onion	bay leaf
whole cloves	parsley
garlic	brown beef stock*
salt and pepper	pan sauce† from a pork roast
Polish sausage	pan sauce† from a lamb roast
butter	previously cooked pork
oil	previously cooked lamb
tomato paste	bread crumbs
Dijon mustard	parsley

Since this famous bean stew requires both pork and lamb that have been prepared in advance you will be able to combine precooked meats from two meals in this dish.

Prepare the beans. Soak overnight[1]

1½ cups (375 ml) navy or Great Northern beans.

After soaking place the beans in a kettle with:

1 medium onion stuck with
2 whole cloves,
1 clove garlic, crushed,
1 tsp. (5 g) salt,
2–3 grinds pepper,
1 or 2 links of Polish sausage.

Simmer the beans for about 2 hours or until they are just tender but remove the sausage after 30 minutes. Reserve the bean cooking liquid for later use when the casserole is finally assembled.

---

[1] There are several options for preparing the beans. Choose the one that best suits your schedule: (1) Soak the beans 2 nights before serving the cassoulet and cook the beans the day before. (2) Begin soaking the beans early in the morning the day before the cassoulet will be served. Simmer the beans later that evening. (3) Shortcut the soaking process. Cover the beans with water. Bring to boil for 2 minutes. Cover the kettle and leave for 1 hour. Proceed with simmering. Once the dish is assembled it may wait for several hours before it is finally baked.

Make the tomato sauce. Cook together slowly for 5 minutes:
>   1 medium onion, chopped,
>   2 Tbs. (30 g) butter.

Add and cook 2 minutes
>   1 large clove garlic, crushed, peeled.

Add and simmer 30 minutes partially covered:
>   2 Tbs. (30 ml) tomato paste,
>   1 tsp. Dijon mustard,
>   pinch thyme,
>   ½ domestic bay leaf,
>   1 sprig parsley, minced,
>   ½ cup (125 ml) beef stock,
>   deglazed pan sauce† from a pork roast,
>   deglazed pan sauce† from a lamb roast.

Preheat the oven 350 F (160 C).

Prepare the meats. Cut up the remains of
>   chilled, previously roasted lamb.

Dry the pieces well on paper towels and brown them very quickly in
>   2 Tbs. (30 ml) hot oil.

Cut up, but do not brown, the remains of
>   chilled, previously roasted pork.

Slice the Polish sausage that was cooked with the beans.

Assemble the dish. Place in a heavy casserole
>   a layer of beans, then
>   a layer of meats (lamb, pork, sausage);
>   repeat, alternating layers, ending with beans on top.

Pour the tomato sauce over the beans and meats in the casserole. Add the bean cooking liquid up to the top layer of beans. Sprinkle the top with
>   fine dry bread crumbs.

Dot over the top
>   1–2 Tbs. (15-30 g) butter.

Bake in the preheated oven for 40 minutes. After removing from the oven, sprinkle over the top
>   2 sprigs parsley, chopped.

Serve. Accompany the cassoulet with a green salad and French bread and serve it from the casserole.

Wine Guide. Select a Burgundy or one of its varietals.

COVER ROASTED PORK CHOPS

Ingredients

pork chops (or steaks)	celery
pork marinade,* if desired	thyme
oil	bay leaf
carrot	parsley
onion	dry white wine or brown beef stock*

Pork chops (or pork steaks) may be marinated; or, proceed without any preliminaries.

Preheat the oven 325 F (150 C).

Brown the chops. Dry the chops well on paper towels and brown them quickly in

1 Tbs. (15 ml) oil.

Only do as many as can comfortably fit in the bottom of a heavy casserole. When all chops have been browned on both sides, pour out all but ½ Tbs. (8 ml) fat. Stir in and cook a moment on low heat:

½ medium carrot, sliced,
½ medium onion, sliced.

Return the chops to the casserole in one overlapping layer. Add a bouquet of herbs:

1 small stalk celery,
pinch thyme,
¼ domestic bay leaf,
2 sprigs parsley.

Cover the casserole and complete the cooking of the chops in the preheated oven for 30 minutes. After 15 minutes of cooking turn the chops and baste them. When the chops are done remove them from the casserole to a hot platter.

Complete the sauce. To deglaze the casserole pour in

½ cup (125 ml) dry white wine or beef stock.

Simmer a moment, scraping the pan to incorporate the browned drippings. Spoon this sauce over the chops and serve.

Wine Guide. Select a white Rhine wine or one of its varietals.

PORK RIBS IN RED WINE MARINADE

Ingredients

pork ribs	fennel seeds
red wine	parsley
garlic	oil
salt and pepper	

Marinate the ribs. Cut into serving-size sections

ribs from a loin of pork.

Mix the marinade ingredients in a shallow glass or enamel pan:

½ cup (125 ml) dry red wine,
1-2 cloves garlic, crushed, peeled,
2 grinds pepper,
¼ tsp. fennel seeds, crushed,
¼ tsp. salt,
1 sprig parsley, chopped,
1 Tbs. (15 ml) oil.

Add the ribs and marinate them for 2 or 3 hours, turning and basting them several times.

Preheat the oven 450 F (210 C).

Roast the ribs. Lift the ribs from the marinade and dry them well on paper towels. Place them in a roasting pan and sear them in the hot preheated oven for 15 minutes. Reduce the heat to 325 F (150 C) and continue to cook them for 1 hour. In this final phase, baste the ribs twice with the marinade.

Serve. Accompany these Italian-flavored pork ribs with risotto* or buttered fettuccini noodles.

Wine Guide. Choose a Chablis, a Claret, one of their varietals, or a Beaujolais.

Ham

This section contains recipes for mild-cured, fully cooked ham, the kind most widely available in this country. The entire ham is first blanched and then braised to eliminate the cure's excessive saltiness. The Madeira sauce accompanying the first presentation is less sweet than American style glazes and couples well with the smoky flavor of the meat.

Several recipes utilize slices of ham in secondary meals after the initial cooking. The first recipes call for slices, the later ones for the irregular pieces at the shank end. A large ham may be divided after the initial braising, packaged (each labeled with its intended purpose), and frozen. Included are many suggestions for serving ham in a variety of fresh and appealing ways.

BRAISED HAM WITH MADEIRA SAUCE ███████████████████

Ingredients

carrots	whole cloves, optional
onion	Madeira
celery	brown beef stock*
parsley	sauce Espagnole*
ham	

Prepare the stock for the initial blanching. Simmer together for 15 minutes:

4–5 qts. (4-5 l) water,
2 carrots, sliced,
1 onion, sliced,
1 large stalk of celery,
3 sprigs parsley.

Add to the stock after it has simmered
ham, about 8 lbs. (3.5-5 kg).

Add more water if necessary to nearly cover the ham. Bring to the simmer and cook slowly for 1 hour.

Preheat the oven 325 F (150 C).

Prepare the ham for braising. Remove the ham to a cutting board. Peel off the rind; trim off the excess fat leaving a ¼-inch (.5 cm) layer. Score the fat in a diamond pattern and, if desired, stud the ham with a few whole cloves.

Place the ham in a roasting pan.

Braise the ham. Pour over:

   1 cup (250 ml) Madeira,
   ½ cup (125 ml) brown beef stock.

Cover the roasting pan and set it in the preheated oven for half an hour, basting twice during that period.

Final glazing. Remove the cover and cook for 30 minutes longer, basting 3 times.

Make the Madeira sauce. Remove the ham from the pan. Skim the fat from the pan juices. Boil down if necessary to ¾ cup (180 ml). Blend the reduced pan juices with

   1 cup (250 ml) sauce Espagnole.

Cook down a little to make a light sauce.

Serve. Slice the ham and ladle over each serving a spoonful or two of the Madeira sauce.

Wine Guide. Select a Chablis, a Claret, or one of their varietals.

SLICES OF HAM IN MADEIRA SAUCE WITH CREAM ▰▰▰▰▰▰▰▰▰▰

Ingredients

Madeira sauce (above)	cream
Cognac	braised spinach*
tomato paste	slices of previously braised
pepper	ham

Convert the sauce. Blend together in a skillet and heat to a slow boil:

   1 cup (250 ml) Madeira sauce,
   2 Tbs. (30 ml) Cognac,
   1 Tbs. tomato paste,
   2 grinds of pepper.

Reduce the heat. Simmer a few minutes, stirring to blend the flavors. Blend in

   ½ cup (125 ml) cream.

Add the ham. Gently reheat in this sauce
   slices of braised ham.

Serve. Arrange the slices of ham on a platter of
   braised spinach.

Pour some of the sauce over the ham and serve the remainder in a sauce dish.

Wine Guide. Choose a Chablis or one of its varietals.

SLICES OF HAM WITH CHICKEN SUPRÊMES IN PAPER HEARTS ███████████

Ingredients

breast of chicken	lemon
slices of previously braised ham	salt and pepper
	flour
typing paper	butter
mushroom,* cream* or Mornay sauce*	dry white wine

Each serving containing slices of ham, a section of boneless breast of chicken, and a complementary sauce is cooked and served in a sealed, heart-shaped paper case. The use of paper cases is a variation on the insulated reheating principle. It prevents overheating while blending the flavors of ham, chicken, and sauce. Amounts given below are for 4 servings, but may be increased proportionally.

Bone the chicken breasts. This may be accomplished well in advance, even the day before cooking. For each 4 servings use

1 whole breast of a chicken (both sides).

Pull off the skin from the breast. Working carefully with a short, sharp, pointed knife and starting at the bone which separates the two sides of the breast, cut away the meat from one side in one, intact piece. Repeat with the other side of the breast. Examine the cut undersides of the meat. Each piece of breast meat has a white filament (tendon) running lengthwise into the meat. Pull it against the blade of the knife to remove it. Flatten the suprêmes (boneless breasts of chicken) somewhat with the flat side of a broad-bladed knife and trim up any jagged edges. Cut each piece in two, making 4 equal sizes of breast meat. Each piece should be approximately 3x4 inches (7.5x10 cm). Cover and refrigerate until cooking.

Slice the ham. Cut

8 slices of braised ham measuring 3x4x¼ inches (7.5x10x.5 cm).

Two slices will be used for each serving.

Make the paper hearts for cases. Select a good quality paper such as

8 sheets of bond typing paper, 8½x11 inches (21x27.5 cm).

Fold them in half so that the folded size is 8½x5½ inches (21x14 cm). For uniformity cut them all from the same pattern, trimming away three corners to make a heart shape. Two hearts will be used for each serving case.

Prepare the sauce. Choose a variation of béchamel

mushroom, cream, or Mornay sauce.

Preheat the oven 400 F (185 C).

Sauté the chicken suprêmes. Rub each piece of prepared, boneless breast of chicken with

> drops of lemon juice.

Season lightly to taste with

> salt and pepper.

Dip the chicken lightly in

> flour sifted onto a plate.

Melt in a heavy skillet over medium-high heat

> 3 Tbs. (45 g) butter.

When the butter foams and begins to subside add the pieces of chicken breast. Take care that the butter does not burn; tilt and roll the pan every few moments while cooking. Sauté the chicken about 3 minutes on each side. Watch the process closely to prevent its overcooking. The suprême is done when the meat is resistant to the pressure of the forefinger, but not yet firm. (If, however, it feels soft to the touch more cooking is required.) Remove the sautéed breast pieces as soon as they are done to a side dish and pour out the fat from the pan. Deglaze† the skillet with

> ¼ cup (60 ml) dry white wine.

Scrape up the browned bits in the pan to incorporate them. When the liquid has reduced to half pour it into the prepared sauce.

Assemble the cases for reheating. Bring the sauce to simmering. Butter one side of each of the paper hearts. Place 4 hearts on a baking tray, buttered side up. On each heart place in the order given:

> slice of ham,
> 1-2 spoonfuls of sauce,
> piece of sautéed chicken breast,
> 1-2 spoonfuls of sauce,
> slice of ham,
> paper heart, buttered side down.

Seal the heart cases. Beginning at the point and progressing all the way around the heart, roll the edges together in 2 or 3 quarter-inch (half-centimeter) folds until the cases are completely sealed.

Reheat. Place the baking sheet with the sealed cases in the hot pre-heated oven for 5 or 6 minutes until the paper begins to brown.

Serve. Place each heart on a serving plate. With a pointed knife cut the tops of the cases open in a wide "V." Serve at once while very hot.

Wine Guide. Select a Chablis or one of its varietals.

SLICES OF HAM IN TOMATO SAUCE ▐▬▬▬▬▬▬▬▬▬▬▬▬▬

Ingredients

slices of previously braised ham	green pepper
	hot pepper or cayenne or
tomato sauce*	Tabasco sauce

Convert the sauce. Prepare
  tomato sauce.
Add:
  ¼ of a green pepper, cut in a dice or julienne† strips and blanched†
    3-4 minutes in boiling water,
  ½ of a tiny, hot pepper, slivered, or pinch of cayenne or dash of
    Tabasco.
Gently reheat in the sauce
  slices of previously braised ham.
Wine Guide. Select a Burgundy (generic or varietal).
  Note. Any remaining ham and sauce from this dish makes a good filling
for an omelet.* Dice† the ham into the sauce and fill the omelet in the
usual manner.

CHOUCROÛTE GARNI ▰▰▰▰▰▰▰▰▰▰▰▰▰▰▰▰▰▰▰▰
(Braised Sauerkraut Garnished with Meat)

Ingredients

sauerkraut	dry white wine
bacon	brown beef stock*
butter	pepper
carrot	slices of previously cooked
onion	ham
parsley	sausages: Polish, franks, or
bay leaf	knackwurst

Preheat the oven 325 F (150 C).
  Prepare the sauerkraut. If you like the briny flavor of sauerkraut,
simply squeeze it dry from the jar; otherwise, if you prefer a much milder
flavor, drain, rinse in cold water and then squeeze dry
  2 lbs. (1 kg) sauerkraut packed in a refrigerated jar (not canned).
  Assemble the casserole. Blanch by simmering 10 minutes
  3 slices bacon in
  1 qt. (1 l) water.
Cook together in a heavy casserole, slowly for 10 minutes:
  the blanched bacon, drained, rinsed, dried and each slice cut into
    about 8 crosscut pieces,
  1 Tbs. (15 g) butter,
  1 medium carrot, sliced,
  1 medium onion, sliced.
Stir in the sauerkraut. Add the herbs:
  2 sprigs parsley,
  ⅓ domestic bay leaf.
Season lightly with
  pepper.

Pour in
> ⅓ cup (80 ml) dry white wine and enough beef stock to just cover
> the sauerkraut.

Cut a piece of brown paper the size of the inside of the casserole. Butter the paper and lay it over the sauerkraut.

Bake the casserole. Place in the preheated oven and cook very slowly for 1½ hours. Remove the brown paper and arrange over the top of the sauerkraut:
> slices of ham,
> browned sausages.

Continue cooking for 30 minutes.

Serve. Accompany with boiled potatoes.

Wine Guide. Select a Chablis if the sauerkraut was rinsed in water before cooking. If it was not, choose a sturdier Claret or Burgundy.

Note. A browned pork roast, chops, or a duckling may finish their cooking over the sauerkraut. Consult those sections for details.

SERVING SUGGESTIONS FOR IRREGULAR PIECES OF HAM

(1) *Crêpes filling.* Combine julienne† strips of ham and Swiss cheese. Roll inside crêpes and arrange in a buttered casserole dish. Cover them with béchamel sauce,* grated Swiss cheese, and dots of butter. Reheat at serving time in the upper level of a 375 F (170 C) oven for 30 minutes. These may also be cut in half to be used as hot hors d'oeuvre.

(2) *Soufflé.* Following the basic outline,* use any of the following combinations to flavor the base: (a) ¾ cup (180 ml) minced ham and ½ cup (125 ml) grated Swiss cheese; (b) 1½ cups (375 ml) chopped ham; (c) 1 cup (250 ml) chopped ham and ½ cup (125 ml) chopped chicken.

(3) Substitute ground ham for pork in the stuffing for Beef Rolls.*

(4) *Sauce Espagnole.* Simmer, drain, rinse, and chop a small piece of ham. Use to season this brown sauce.

(5) *Pasta Fazool.* Add the bone and a few pieces to cook with the beans.

(6) Or, finish up the last pieces of ham in the following pie which is similar to a quiche.

HAM AND POTATO PIE

Ingredients

puréed potatoes*	butter
cottage cheese	onion
eggs	pieces of ham, previously
parsley	cooked
salt and pepper	unbaked pastry shell*
nutmeg	
cream	

Preheat the oven 350 F (160 C).

Prepare the filling. Blend together in a bowl:

    1 cup (250 ml) puréed potatoes (may be left over from another meal),

    1 cup (250 ml) cottage cheese,

    3 eggs, beaten,

    2 sprigs parsley, minced,

    ½ tsp. salt,

    1-2 grinds pepper,

    pinch nutmeg,

    1-2 Tbs. (15-30 ml) cream.

Sauté in a small skillet until transparent:

    1 Tbs. (15 g) butter,

    ½ small onion, minced.

Stir in

    ½ cup (125 ml) ham cut in a small dice.

Add the onion and ham to the bowl and fold into the potato mixture.

Final steps. Pour the filling mixture into an

    8-inch (20 cm) unbaked pie shell.

Dot over the top

    ½ Tbs. (8 g) butter.

Bake in the preheated oven for 45 minutes until lightly browned on top and puffed like a quiche.

Wine Guide. Select a Chablis or one of its varietals.

Salmon Trout

Fish preparation may appear to have been cursorily treated, having been given only one section. But a close examination will show that the basic methods are flexible and have wide application. The techniques applied to salmon work well with many other fish. If it is not to be sautéed (that is, dipped first in milk, then in flour, and browned lightly on each side in hot butter and oil) then it can probably be treated in one of the ways explained in this section. The essential point when cooking any fish is to watch closely so it cooks only until just done.

For the following recipes, a large salmon trout was used. Steaks were sliced from the large end and the remainder was poached. Depending on the amount remaining, there are numerous suggestions given for incorporating the once-poached salmon and its cooking liquid in secondary dishes.

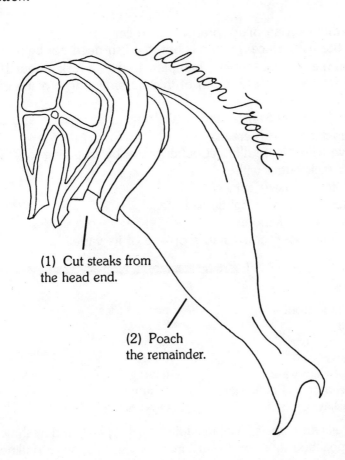

Salmon Trout

(1) Cut steaks from
the head end.

(2) Poach
the remainder.

Broiled Salmon Steaks

Ingredients

> salmon steaks
> salt and pepper
> butter
> vinaigrette (sauce) with cream* or
>   Maitre d'Hotel butter (below)

Preheat the broiler pan under the broiler.

Prepare the fish. Besides salmon, boneless filet of cod, sole, perch, or halibut, and various small trout may be broiled and sauced in this way. Season lightly:

> salmon steaks removed from the end of a large trout with
> salt.

(Other fish less fatty than salmon should also be given a light dusting of flour at this point.) Brush the steaks with

> melted butter.

Place them on an oiled, preheated broiler pan.

Broil the fish. Since the pan is hot, the fish need not be turned. Cook only until the fish are tender when pierced with a fork, about 10 minutes (or less) for each inch (2.5 cm) of thickness. During broiling baste twice with melted butter.

Serve. Carefully transfer the steaks onto a hot platter and serve with
vinaigrette with cream
or serve with Maitre d'Hôtel butter made by creaming together:
½ stick butter with
1 sprig parsley, minced,
salt and pepper lightly to taste,
juice of ¼ lemon.
Wine Guide. Select a Chablis or one of its varietals.

POACHED SALMON TROUT ▬▬▬▬▬▬▬▬▬▬▬▬▬▬▬▬▬▬

Ingredients

salmon trout	peppercorns
salt	bay leaf
lemon juice	thyme
water	butter
dry white wine	flour
green onions or shallots	cream
parsley	cheesecloth

Practically any type of fish, including steaks, filets, and fresh water trout may be poached in a court bouillon† following the steps outlined below. As a general rule allow 10 minutes of cooking time for each inch (2.5 cm) of the fish's thickness. Shellfish may be cooked this way but it is better to place them on a rack above the aromatic bouillon and steam until done.

Initial marination. Unless the fish is absolutely fresh, marinate the salmon trout for half-an-hour turning it once in:
salt, a light sprinkling,
juice of ½ to 1 lemon, as required, depending on the size of the fish.
Preheat the oven 350 F (160 C).
Wash the fish well under running water.
Make a court bouillon (for a poaching liquid). Simmer together for 10 minutes:
1½ cups (375 ml) water,
½ cup (125 ml) dry white wine,
2 green onions or shallots, minced,
1 sprig of parsley,
½ tsp. salt,
2 peppercorns,
¼ domestic bay leaf,
pinch thyme.

Poach the fish. Melt in a casserole large enough to hold the fish
   1 Tbs. (15 g) butter.
Lay a piece of cheesecloth in the casserole (to facilitate removal since cooked salmon breaks easily). Place the salmon on the cloth. Strain the court bouillon and pour over the fish. Bring to a simmer on the top of the stove. Cover the casserole and bake in the preheated oven counting about 10 minutes of cooking time for each inch (2.5 cm) of thickness. Baste several times and cook only until the fish is tender when tested with a fork.

Prepare for serving. With the aid of the cheesecloth, carefully lift the fish onto a hot serving platter and remove the skin and dark meat from the side that is up. By lifting one edge of the cheesecloth, turn the fish over. Take away the cloth and remove the skin and dark meat from the other side. Keep it hot by laying a clean towel over the fish and platter.

Make the Velouté sauce. Melt in a saucepan
   1 Tbs. (15 g) butter.
Blend in and cook until just beginning to brown
   1 Tbs. (15 g) flour.
Pour in and cook until lightly thickened and somewhat reduced
   1 cup (250 ml) hot poaching liquid, strained.
Season by blending in:
   1-2 Tbs. (15-30 ml) cream,
   few drops of lemon juice, to taste,
   salt and pepper, to taste.

Serve. Cut the "up" side of the trout into sections and carefully lift them off the bones. Ladle a spoonful or two of the sauce over each serving. When the upper half of the fish has been served, lift off the entire bony skeleton and divide the meat of the other side.

Wine Guide. Select a generic Chablis or a varietal of that group.

PROCEDURES FOR UTILIZING POACHED SALMON

Divide the remaining fish and sauce according to the requirements of the dishes you have in mind and the amount remaining.

(1) *Tart filling* (see below): reserve 1 cup (250 ml) poached, flaked salmon and ¼ cup (60 ml) poaching liquid.

(2) *Macaroni dish* (below): 1 cup or 250 ml (or more) salmon and ¼ cup (60 ml) poaching liquid.

(3) *Soufflé*: ¾ cup or 180 ml (or a little less) of salmon and ¼ cup (60 ml) poaching liquid (outlined below).

(4) *Crêpes filling*: A little salmon may be folded into any Velouté sauce that is left. It may be combined with grated Swiss cheese and seasoned with a pinch of marjoram, basil, or oregano. For crêpe making procedure consult Index.

SALMON TART WITH PEAS ▰▰▰▰▰▰▰▰▰▰▰▰▰▰▰▰▰▰▰▰▰▰▰▰

Ingredients

pastry shell,* optional	dry white wine
butter	salt and pepper
onion	oregano
flour	basil
milk	cream
salmon, previously poached	peas
salmon poaching liquid	Swiss cheese

This filling may be baked in a shallow dish but it is especially good when baked in a pastry.

Prepare in advance
8-inch (20 cm) partially baked pie shell.

Preheat the oven 425 F (200 C).

Make the filling. Cook together over low heat without browning:
3 Tbs. (45 g) butter,
½ small onion, minced.

Stir in and cook 1 to 2 minutes (bubbling, without browning)
3 Tbs. (45 g) flour.

Take off the heat and pour in
1 cup (250 ml) boiling milk.

Return to the heat; boil, whisking for a few seconds. Add:
¼ cup (60 ml) salmon poaching liquid,
1 Tbs. (15 ml) dry white wine,
¼ tsp. salt,
1–2 grinds of pepper,
¼ tsp. oregano,
¼ tsp. basil.

Cook several more minutes until quite thickened. Thin out with
¼ cup (60 ml) cream.

Fold in:
1 cup (250 ml) cooked salmon, flaked,
½ cup (125 ml) frozen peas, defrosted.

Turn into the pastry shell. Sprinkle over the top:
grated Swiss cheese,
dots of butter.

Bake the tart. Place on an upper rack of a hot preheated oven. Bake for 15 minutes or until the top is lightly browned.

Wine Guide. Select a Rhine, a Chablis, or one of their varietals.

SALMON WITH MACARONI ████████████████████

Ingredients

butter	shell macaroni
flour	Swiss cheese
milk	poached salmon
salt and pepper	salmon poaching liquid

Preheat the oven 350 F (160 C).
Make the sauce base. Prepare a thick béchamel* in these proportions:
2½ Tbs. (40 g) butter,
2½ Tbs. (40 g) flour,
1 cup (250 ml) milk.
Prepare the pasta. Cook al dente†
4 oz. (120 g) shell macaroni.
Drain the macaroni well and blend into it:
3 Tbs. (45 ml) of the béchamel sauce base, prepared above,
3 Tbs. (45 ml) grated Swiss cheese (also grate 1 additional spoonful
for the garnish).
Complete the sauce. Add to the remaining sauce base and blend with a
wire whip to smooth
¼ cup (60 ml) salmon poaching liquid.
Assemble the casserole. Turn the macaroni into a buttered casserole.
Arrange over the macaroni
pieces of salmon, previously cooked, skinned and boned.
Pour the sauce over the salmon and sprinkle the remaining spoonful of
cheese over the top. Bake in the preheated oven for 15 minutes. Serve
immediately.
Wine Guide. Select a Rhine wine (generic or varietal).

SALMON SOUFFLÉ ████████████████████

Ingredients

butter	tomato paste
flour	marjoram
milk	salmon, poached
onion	Swiss cheese
poaching liquid	eggs
salt and pepper	

Preheat the oven 400 F (185 C).
Follow the procedure for making the basic soufflé.*
Adapt the base. For a salmon soufflé, cook with the butter
½ small onion, minced.

For the hot liquid use:
>   1 cup (250 ml) boiling milk,
>   ¼ cup (60 ml) poaching liquid added *after* the milk has been
>   blended and cooked with the roux.†

Season the base with:
>   ½ tsp. salt,
>   1–2 grinds pepper,
>   1 Tbs. tomato paste,
>   ½ tsp. marjoram.

For the purée† use:
>   1 scant cup (about 250 ml) salmon, puréed or finely chopped,
>   ½ cup (125 ml) grated Swiss cheese.

Wine Guide. Select a Chablis, a Rhine wine, or one of their varietals.

SERVING SUGGESTIONS FOR FISH

(1) *Fish in tomato sauce.* A notable omission from this section is a tomato-based poaching sauce used for deep sea fish, but which is not particularly compatible with salmon. Combine tomato sauce* (or the Mediterranean variation) with ⅔ cup (160 ml) dry white wine. Use it for poaching† tuna, halibut, swordfish, and red snapper.

(2) *Deep-fried fish.* Serving-size blocks of boned fish such as cod and perch, shelled shrimp, and scallops may be batter-coated* and deep-fried.*

(3) *Sauced fish.* Pieces of salmon and other cooked fish may be arranged in a casserole dish, sauced, and finished exactly like Chicken Mornay.*

(4) *Fish croquettes.* Follow the method for Veal Croquettes.* A flavorful addition to the sauce base is sautéed mushrooms* or duxelles.*

Chicken

There are so many possibilities for chicken. In this section a chicken is prepared three primary ways. It is (A) roasted (in an open pan in the oven); (B) sautéed (in a skillet on top of the stove); and (C) fricasséed (in a closed casserole with liquid). Following the recipe for each primary method is a suggestion for using the remains in a secondary dish that is particularly suitable for that method.

Essentially, every method of initial cooking and utilizing previously cooked meats developed in preceding sections may be applied to chicken. The closing notes refer to other adaptable ideas that are described more fully elsewhere in the book. The flexibility of chicken cookery enables us to draw together many threads and present them here, at the conclusion of the chapter on meats, in a summary weave of cooking methods.

(A) Roasted Chicken

ROASTED CHICKEN WITH STUFFING AND PAN SAUCE ██████████████

Ingredients

chicken and giblets	thyme	dried bread
onions	bay leaf	marjoram
whole clove	salt and pepper	butcher string
carrots	butter	small skewer
celery	dry white wine	
parsley	Cognac	

Make a simple stock. This stock may be made at any time, before or during the chicken's roasting. It will be used to make the sauce to accompany the roasted chicken. Simmer together for 1 hour or longer:

the giblets of a 3½ lb. (1.5 kg) chicken,

½ small onion, stuck with

1 whole clove,

½ small carrot,

water to cover,

dash of salt.

Add a bouquet of herbs:

1 stalk celery,

2 sprigs parsley,

pinch thyme,

¼ domestic bay leaf.

Preheat the oven 375 F (170 C).

Prepare the stuffing. English style (bread) stuffing. Cook together gently for 3 to 4 minutes without browning:

3 Tbs. (45 g) butter,

½ small onion, minced,

1 small carrot, finely diced,

½ stalk celery, finely diced.

Stir in and boil slowly to reduce the liquid to half

1 Tbs. each (30 ml total) dry white wine and Cognac.

Fold in and blend well:

½ cup (125 ml) crumbs from dried (but not toasted) French bread,

3 sprigs parsley, minced,

salt and pepper, lightly to taste,

¼ tsp. each thyme and marjoram.

Prepare the bird for roasting. Season the inside of the chicken lightly with

salt.

Fill the cavity loosely with the stuffing. Sew or skewer the vent in order to close it enough to retain the stuffing; then, truss the chicken. This may be done without sewing; tie the legs together in the middle of a long string. Hook the wing tips behind the back. Run the string along each side of the body over the wings and under to the back, drawing the string tightly to bring the legs and wings close to the body. Tie underneath.

Roast the chicken. Rub the skin with

2 Tbs. (30 g) softened butter.

Place it in a roasting pan on a bed of vegetables:

1 medium onion, sliced,

1 medium carrot, sliced.

Set the pan in the middle level of the preheated oven and roast first on one side, then on the other, about 12 minutes on each side.

Reset the oven to 350 F (160 C).

Rest the chicken on its back (breast up) and finish roasting. Baste it often with the butter in the pan, about every 10 minutes, for 1 to 1½ hours.

Determine doneness. A roasted chicken is done at the moment its juices run clear yellow when the thickest part of the drumstick is pricked. The drumstick will also feel tender when pressed and will move easily in its joint.

Make the sauce. Pour out the fat from the roasting pan. Add

1 cup (250 ml) of the previously made chicken giblet stock, strained.

Boil the stock down a little, scraping up the pan juices to incorporate them into the sauce. Lift out the vegetables with a slotted spoon just before serving and add:

salt and pepper to correct the seasoning,

½ Tbs. (8 g) butter, optional.

Serve. Spoon the stuffing into a separate dish and carve the bird. Accompany each serving with a spoonful of stuffing and of sauce.

Wine Guide. Select a Chablis, a Claret, or one of their varietals.

Note. After dinner, remove the meat from the chicken. Crush the carcass a bit and return it to a kettle with a scraped, quartered carrot, a peeled and quartered onion, a bouquet of herbs† and celery, ½ tsp. salt, and water to cover. Let it simmer a few hours to make a stock* for soup.

SPLIT PEA SOUP ██

Ingredients

butter	pan sauce,† if available
onion	salt and pepper
carrot	tomato
celery	boiled ham or shredded,
bacon	cooked chicken, optional
dried, split peas	cream
chicken stock previously	croutons, sautéed in butter
simmered from the carcass	
(see note above)	

Prepare the seasonings. Cook together slowly in a heavy, deep-sided casserole:

    2 Tbs. (30 g) butter,

    2 Tbs. (30 ml) each: onion, carrot, celery, finely diced,

    3 slices bacon simmered 10 minutes in 1 qt. (1 l) water; drained, rinsed, dried, chopped.

Stir in

    1½ cups (375 ml) dried, split peas.

Pour over:

    1 qt. (1 l) chicken stock,

    2-3 Tbs. (30–43 ml) pan sauce from roasted chicken, if available, for additional flavor.

Season with:

    ½ tsp. salt,

    1-3 grinds of pepper.

Cook the soup. Bring the soup almost to a boil, skimming off the foam with a slotted spoon as it rises to the top. Reduce the heat to simmer. Place a lid on the casserole but allow a wide vent for steam to escape. Cook the peas gently for 1 hour.

Purée† the peas. Remove about 1 cup (250 ml) of the peas and return the purée to the pot with:

    1 tomato, peeled, seeded, chopped,

    diced or shredded boiled ham or cooked,

      diced chicken, optional.

Continue simmering the soup for 15–20 minutes. At the last moment taste for seasoning and blend in

    ½ cup (125 ml) cream.

Serve. Garnish with

    croutons sautéed in butter until lightly browned.

Wine Guide. Wine should have enough character to stand up to the soup without competing with its slightly sweet flavor. Select a light Chablis or light Burgundy such as Green Hungarian or Mountain Burgundy.

CHICKEN RAVIOLI

Ingredients

ground, cooked chicken	chicken stock* or pan sauce†
salt and pepper	flour
parsley	salt
butter	eggs
garlic	cream
Swiss cheese	tomato sauce,* optional

Roasted chicken tends to become dry with reheating. If it is not used cold in salads, it may be successfully reheated if it has been ground. As a tasty filling for ravioli, it will not suffer from overcooking. This recipe could be used as the main dish for an informal party (from "leftovers"!).

Make the filling. Combine in a bowl:
  ¾ cup (185 ml) ground, cooked chicken,
  salt and pepper, to taste,
  2 sprigs parsley, minced.
Sauté together without browning:
  1 Tbs. (15 g) butter,
  1 clove garlic, crushed, peeled.
Scrape the garlic and butter into the bowl; also add
  ¼ cup (60 ml) grated Swiss cheese (pressed down to measure).
Add to the mixture by spoonfuls blending in enough to make a heavy paste
  chicken stock or deglazed pan sauce† skimmed of fat.
Make the egg noodle dough. Sift into a bowl:
  2 cups (8 oz. or 225 g) sifted flour,
  1 tsp. (5 g) salt.
Beat together:
  2 eggs,
  ¼ cup (60 ml) cream.
Pour the eggs and cream into the flour and gradually blend together by beating with a large fork. The dough must be stiff. If necessary add more flour. Roll the dough out as thinly as possible on a floured board. Allow it to rest 20 minutes.

Shape the ravioli. Cut the egg noodle dough into circular shapes with a biscuit cutter or a glass rim with a 2½-inch (6 cm) diameter. Place a small spoonful of chicken filling just off-center on each of the circles. Fold each in half to resemble a turnover. Dip your finger in water and run it around the lower semi-circle edge of the ravioli. Press the upper half firmly into the moistened lower edge. Press the seam with the tines of a fork to seal. Let the ravioli dry for at least 2 hours, turning them over from time to time. The ravioli may then be frozen separately, stored in a plastic bag, and taken out as needed.

Boiling the ravioli. Drop the ravioli into a large kettle of rapidly boiling water. When tender drain the ravioli in a colander.

Preheat the oven 375 F (170 C).

Final baking (two methods). (1) Layer the ravioli in a buttered casserole with dots of butter between layers and Swiss cheese grated over the top. Bake until the butter is melted, the ravioli heated through, and the cheese on top lightly browned.

(2) Or, combine the ravioli with a tomato sauce. Sprinkle grated Swiss cheese over the top and bake until heated through, about half an hour.

Wine Guide. Select a Chablis, a Claret, or one of their varietals.

CHICKEN SALAD ▬▬▬▬▬▬▬▬▬▬▬▬▬▬▬▬

Ingredients

rice, previously cooked
chicken, previously cooked
fresh lemon juice
cream
Dijon mustard
salt and pepper
parsley
other fresh herbs, if available

asparagus tips, previously
  cooked
hard-boiled eggs
chicken liver pâté* or a good
  canned variety
watercress
lettuce

Initial preparations. Combine, preferably while the rice is still warm:
  2 cups (500 ml) cooked rice,
  1 cup (250 ml) cooked chicken, diced.
Make the sauce. Beat together until thickened:
  1 Tbs. (15 ml) fresh lemon juice,
  3 Tbs. (45 ml) cream,
  ½ tsp. Dijon mustard,
  salt and pepper lightly to taste,
  1 sprig parsley, minced,
  other fresh herbs, if available, minced.
Fold the sauce into the chicken and rice.
Compose the salad. Arrange on a platter
  lettuce leaves to cover the platter.
Mound the chicken and rice in the center and garnish with:
  asparagus tips, previously cooked,
  sieved yolk of 2-3 hard-boiled eggs.
Fill the whites of the eggs with
  chicken liver pâté.
Bank the stuffed eggs against the chicken and rice. Tuck in
  small bunches of watercress.
Wine Guide. Select a Chablis or one of its varietals.

(B) Sautéed Chicken

SAUTÉED CHICKEN BERCY ▬▬▬▬▬▬▬▬▬

Ingredients

chicken
flour, optional
butter
salt and pepper

green onion or shallot
dry white wine
chicken stock*
parsley

Prepare the chicken. Following the illustration in this section, cut up a
  3½ lb. (1.5 kg) chicken.
Coat the pieces, if desired, in
  flour.
Shake off any excess.
Sauté the chicken. Melt in a heavy skillet over medium heat
  3 Tbs. (45 g) butter.
Add the pieces of chicken skin side down and cook until the skin is a
golden color. Turn the pieces over. Season lightly with
  salt and pepper.
Cook, partly covered, over low heat for 20 to 25 minutes. Remove the
white meat and continue to cook the dark meat 5 to 10 minutes longer
until done. Remove the dark meat pieces.
Make the sauce. Pour out all but 1 Tbs. (15 ml) butter from the pan.
Stir into the pan drippings
  1 large shallot or 2 green onions, minced.
Cook-stir a minute and then pour in:
  ¼ cup (60 ml) dry white wine,
  ¼ cup (60 ml) chicken stock.
Cook down rapidly, stirring, until reduced and somewhat thickened.
Season with
  1–2 sprigs parsley, chopped.
Return the chicken pieces to the pan to reheat briefly. Simmer 3 or 4
minutes.
Serve. Arrange the chicken on a hot serving platter and spread the
sauce over the chicken pieces.
Wine Guide. Select a Chablis, a Claret, or one of their varietals.
Variations. (1) Sautéed Chicken Bordelaise. Substitute ⅓ cup (80 ml)
dry red wine for the dry white wine and stock in the sauce.
(2) Sautéed Chicken with Herbs. Sauté the chicken as above in
  4 Tbs. (60 g) butter.
When seasoning with salt and pepper also add:
  ⅛ tsp. fennel seeds,
  ⅛ tsp. thyme
  ¼ tsp. basil.
When making the sauce add to the butter in the pan instead of shallot
  1 large clove garlic, crushed, peeled, finely chopped.
Simmer the garlic a moment; add and boil down to reduce to half
  ½ cup (125 ml) dry white wine or dry red wine.
Garnish with parsley and serve.
Wine Guide. Choose from Chablis, Claret, their varietals, or Beaujolais.

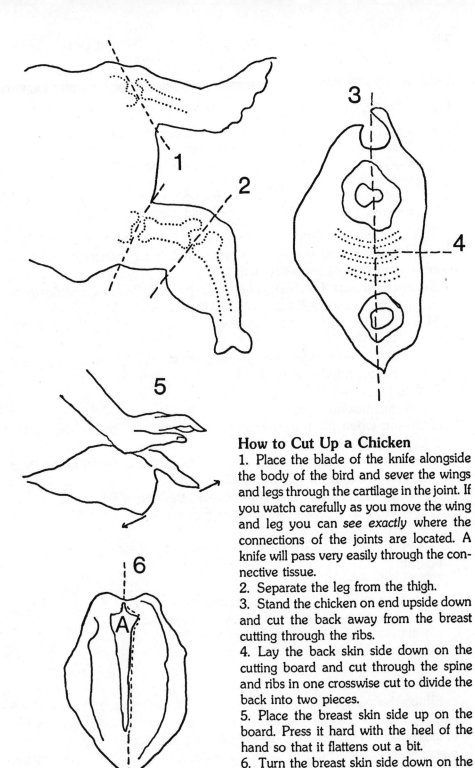

How to Cut Up a Chicken

1. Place the blade of the knife alongside the body of the bird and sever the wings and legs through the cartilage in the joint. If you watch carefully as you move the wing and leg you can *see exactly* where the connections of the joints are located. A knife will pass very easily through the connective tissue.

2. Separate the leg from the thigh.

3. Stand the chicken on end upside down and cut the back away from the breast cutting through the ribs.

4. Lay the back skin side down on the cutting board and cut through the spine and ribs in one crosswise cut to divide the back into two pieces.

5. Place the breast skin side up on the board. Press it hard with the heel of the hand so that it flattens out a bit.

6. Turn the breast skin side down on the board and separate it lengthwise, cutting away the thick breast bone (A) as you go.

ENGLISH CHICKEN PASTY ████████████████████████████████

Ingredients

pastry*	chicken stock* or pan sauce†
butter	vinegar
bacon	Worcestershire sauce
mushrooms	parsley
onions	previously cooked chicken
eggs	salt and pepper

This savory combination provides a good background for the flavor of sautéed chicken and the meat is prevented from overcooking by the double insulation of its pastry wrap.

Advance preparation. Make ahead and have chilling in the refrigerator
  pastry,* about half the amount will be used.

Make the filling. Sauté together in a small skillet for 1-2 minutes:
  1 Tbs. (15 g) butter,
  3 slices bacon, simmered 10 minutes in 1 qt. (1 l) water; drained, rinsed, dried, chopped.

Add to the skillet
  4 mushrooms, sliced.

Cook-stir; when the mushrooms are just beginning to brown, stir in
  ½ small onion, diced.

Cook until the onion is transparent. Remove the skillet from the heat.
Combine in a bowl and blend until smooth:
  yolks of 2 hard-boiled eggs pressed through a fine sieve,
  ¼ cup (60 ml) chicken stock or pan sauce,
  2 tsp. vinegar,
  ½ tsp. Worcestershire sauce.

Fold in:
  1 sprig parsley,
  whites of 2 hard-boiled eggs, chopped,
  1–1½ cups (250-375 ml) cooked chicken, diced,
  the sautéed ingredients from the skillet.

Season the combined mixture with
  salt and pepper to taste.

Preheat the oven 425 F (200 C).

Shape the pasty. Roll out the pastry to a circle about 15 inches (37.5 cm) in diameter. Lightly, without actually indenting the pastry, draw a line to indicate the diameter. Place all the filling on one side of the line. Fold the pastry in half at the marked center to make a very large turnover shape. Lightly moisten the outside edge all around with a little water and "glue" the two sides together. Trim the pastry into a neat half-circle. Seal the edges by pressing with the tines of a fork. Prick the top of the pastry in a decorative manner to vent steam. Very carefully transfer the pasty to a

buttered baking sheet. Bake in the hot preheated oven for 25 minutes.
  Wine Guide. Select a Chablis, Claret, or Beaujolais.

(C) Fricasséed Chicken

Chicken Marengo ▰▰▰▰▰▰▰▰▰▰▰▰▰▰▰▰▰▰▰▰

Ingredients

chicken	tomatoes
oil	Cognac
butter	chicken stock*
mushrooms	dry white wine
garlic	salt and pepper

A fricassée is produced by a braising method. It is usually cooked on top of the stove instead of in the oven.
  Initial preparation. Cut into pieces
    3½ lb. (1.5 kg) chicken (see illustration in the preceding section).
  Melt together in a heavy skillet over medium heat:
    2 Tbs. (30 ml) oil,
    2 Tbs. (30 g) butter.
Add the pieces of chicken skin side down and cook until they are golden. Turn and cook a few moments longer. Remove the chicken to a side dish.
  Begin the sauce. Pour out 1 Tbs. (15 ml) of fat from the pan. Stir in and brown lightly over medium-high heat
    6 mushrooms, sliced.
  Stir in:
    1 clove garlic, crushed, peeled,
    4 medium tomatoes, peeled, seeded, juiced, chopped.
Cover; turn the heat to low and cook for 5 minutes to render the juices. Uncover, raise the heat, and cook-stir to evaporate some of the excess liquid.
  Ignite the Cognac. Heat in a small saucepan
    1 Tbs. (15 ml) Cognac.
  Carefully touch a lighted match to the heated Cognac and when it flames pour it over the tomato sauce. Add in equal parts making ¾ cup (375 ml) liquid in all:
    chicken stock,
    dry white wine.
  Return the chicken to the skillet. Season the chicken and the sauce lightly with
    salt and pepper.
Cover and simmer on low heat on top of the stove until done, about 20-25 minutes.
  Serve. Accompany with risotto.*

PASTA SAUCE WITH CHICKEN ▮▮▮▮▮▮▮▮▮▮▮▮▮▮

Ingredients

butter	Marengo sauce
garlic	chicken previously cooked in
flour	Marengo sauce
parsley	spaghetti
basil	Swiss or Parmesan cheese

Prepare the pasta. Have ready when the sauce is completed
　　8 oz. (225 g) spaghetti cooked al dente† in boiling salted water.
Adapt the sauce. Cook slowly in a heavy sauce pan for 2 or 3 minutes without browning:
　　2 Tbs. (30 g) butter,
　　1-2 cloves garlic, crushed, peeled.
At the same time, heat slightly in another pan
　　the Marengo sauce.
Remove the pieces of chicken from it. Sprinkle over the butter and garlic
　　1 Tbs. (15 g) flour.
Cook slowly 1-2 minutes; pour in the heated Marengo sauce. Stir to blend and thicken; add:
　　1 sprig parsley, minced,
　　1½ tsp. dried basil, crushed.
Final steps. Simmer the sauce slowly while skinning and boning
　　the chicken remaining from the Marengo dish.
Dice† the chicken into ½-inch (1 cm) pieces and fold them into the sauce. Continue to simmer, without covering, to reheat the chicken.
Serve. Pour the sauce over the spaghetti arranged on a platter. Pass separately
　　Swiss or Parmesan cheese, grated.
Wine Guide. Choose a Chablis or Beaujolais.
Variation. Capilotade. Do not dice the chicken. Instead, keep the chicken as nearly intact as possible when removing it from the bone. Convert the sauce as explained above. Transfer the sauce and heated chicken onto a serving dish and garnish with
　　croutons, sautéed in butter until lightly browned.

CHICKEN FRICASSÉE, FRENCH STYLE ▮▮▮▮▮▮▮▮▮▮▮

Ingredients

chicken	sugar
salt and pepper	parsley
butter	cream
carrots	Cognac
onions	

Prepare the chicken. Cut up
    3½ lb. (1.5 kg) chicken.
Rub the skin with a little
    flour.
Season the pieces of chicken lightly with
    salt and pepper.
Melt in a heavy skillet over medium heat
    3 Tbs. (45 g) butter.
Add the chicken pieces skin side down and cook until golden brown. Turn and cook until the other side is browned, about 15 minutes total browning time.

Parboil† **the vegetables.** While the chicken is browning, heat to boiling:
    2 cups (500 ml) water,
    1 tsp. sugar.
Add to the boiling water for 3-5 minutes:
    4 medium carrots, sliced,
    3 small onions, sliced.
Drain the vegetables in a colander.

Finish the fricassée. When the chicken has finished browning, reduce the heat and arrange over the top:
    the parboiled vegetables,
    2 sprigs parsley, chopped.
Pour into the skillet
    1 cup (250 ml) cream.
Nearly cover and cook the chicken very slowly on low heat for 25 or 30 minutes. Remove the chicken onto a hot platter.

Complete the sauce. Pour into the cooking liquid
    1 Tbs. (15 ml) Cognac.
Raise the heat to medium and boil slowly to evaporate the alcohol. Correct the seasoning as necessary with
    salt and pepper.

Serve. Lift the vegetables out of the sauce with a slotted spoon and arrange them on the platter with the chicken. Spoon some of the sauce over the chicken and vegetables and pour the remainder in a sauce dish.

Wine Guide. Select a Chablis or one of its varietals.

CHICKEN GNOCCHI, GAMBA ▰▰▰▰▰▰▰▰▰▰▰▰

Ingredients

milk	salt and pepper
butter	previously cooked chicken
hominy grits	Swiss cheese

    This recipe, too, is my father's invention. The gnocchi is reminiscent of polenta,* but lighter and creamier.

Cook the gnocchi. Bring to boiling
    2 cups (500 ml) milk.
Add and stir until melted
    ¼ cup (112 g) butter.
Slowly stir in
    ½ cup (125 ml) hominy grits.
Return to boiling and continue cooking until the mixture is thickened and smooth like farina. Remove from the heat and season with:
    ½ tsp. salt,
    1-2 grinds pepper.
Complete the gnocchi. Beat on high speed with an electric mixer for 5 minutes. With a spatula quickly fold in
    ½–1 cup (125-250 ml) cooked chicken, diced.
Spread into a buttered 8x8-inch (20x20 cm) square pan and allow to set.
Preheat the oven 400 F (185 C).
Assemble the dish. Cut the congealed gnocchi into squares and place them in a buttered baking dish making 2 layers if necessary. Pour over
    2 Tbs. (30 ml) melted butter.
Sprinkle with
    a generous ½ cup (125 ml) grated Swiss cheese.
Bake in the preheated oven for 30 minutes.
Wine Guide. Select a Chablis or one of its varietals.

ALTERNATE INITIAL COOKING METHODS FOR CHICKEN

(1) *Poached chicken.* In addition to preparing it roasted, sautéed, or fricasséed, chicken may be prepared as outlined in the pot-au-feu section. The oven browning step may be eliminated. Add the chicken pieces, giblets, stock vegetables (1 or 2 per person of each, cut into bite-size pieces), a little salt, and a bouquet of herbs† to gently boiling water. Partially cover and simmer about half an hour until the chicken is just done. Cooked this way, the chicken is usually served with rice and the strained vegetables. The stock may be passed in a sauce dish or a béchamel sauce* may be served instead.

(2) *Closed pan roasted† chicken.* Chicken may be cooked in the manner described for Boneless Roast of Pork.* Truss the chicken and rub the skin well with softened butter. Lightly season the cavity with salt. Place the bird in a buttered casserole on a bed of vegetables and follow the browning procedure for the pork roast. Reduce the heat to 325 F (150 C). Lay a piece of aluminum foil over the chicken. Cover the casserole and roast for 40 to 60 minutes longer until the chicken is done. The pan juices make a sufficient sauce.

(3) *Broiled chicken.* Place chicken pieces on a preheated broiler rack.

Baste with melted butter or oil and turn every 5-8 minutes for about 20-25 minutes. Lower the rack if the skin begins to burn or cook too quickly. Pieces may be previously marinated (and basted with the marinade). Use the lemon juice vinaigrette marinade.* Or, prepare the pieces like the Ribs of Beef Diable,* coating first with mustard sauce and then with bread crumbs and butter. Watch broiling closely to prevent burning.

(4) *Chicken suprêmes.* Their preparation and cooking is described in Slices of Ham in Paper Hearts.*

ALTERNATE SECONDARY PREPARATIONS FOR CHICKEN

(1) *Chicken Mornay.** This recipe may be varied by substituting other sauces derived from béchamel sauce* such as curry* or paprika.*

(2) *Crêpes filling.* Previously cooked chicken may be sauced with béchamel* or any of its variations and combined, if desired, with mushrooms, peas, or cheese.

(3) *Chicken pie.* Combine cooked chicken and vegetables (parboiled† 10 minutes) with a Velouté sauce.* Turn into a pastry shell* and bake until the pastry is a rich, golden brown.

(4) *Chicken casserole.* Using the filling described for chicken pie, turn it into a casserole dish and pipe on decorative borders of duchess potatoes.* This procedure is outlined in Beef Hachis.*

(5) *Chicken soufflé.* Prepare as in Salmon Soufflé.* The tomato paste may be omitted. Chopped or ground chicken added to the soufflé base may be combined with grated Swiss cheese or chopped ham.

(6) *Chicken croquettes.* Any of the variations of béchamel sauce* may be used with chicken. Follow the directions given for Veal Croquettes* for the sauce proportions, coating technique, and frying procedure.

Duckling

As pot-au-feu was offered as an introduction to cooking methods, and chicken as a summary of these methods, Braised Duckling with Orange Sauce represents the culmination and refinement of acquired techniques. It should now be evident that even an haute cuisine dish such as this can be easily accomplished by the "average" cook.

This is a special dish, and no short cuts have been used. The sauce is the essence of its success. The things to strive for are deep flavor and fruitiness without sweetness. Achieving this requires not only a browned duck stock for the orange sauce, but also sauce Espagnole and meat jelly.

Until you have constructed all the parts for the sauce, however, there are other delicious ways a duckling may be prepared. Alternate suggestions are given in notes following the recipe.

Braised Duckling with Orange Sauce ▰▰▰▰▰▰▰▰▰▰

Ingredients

oranges	thyme
duckling with giblets	bay leaf
salt and pepper	dry white wine
oil	sauce Espagnole*
carrot	beef jelly*
onion	Cognac
parsley	butcher string
celery	

Preheat the oven 450 F (210 C).

Prepare the oranges. Drop in boiling water and boil gently for 3 minutes

the zest of 2 oranges (the thin outer layer of the peel which contains the "dots" of oil).

Drain the peel; rinse in cold water and dry. Reserve the juice of one of the oranges for the sauce.

Cut the pith from the outside of the other orange; slice it and set it aside to garnish the finished dish. Cut the blanched zest of one orange into a very fine julienne† and reserve that for the sauce. Insert the other peel inside the body cavity of a

5-5½ lb. (2.5 kg) duckling.

Prepare the duckling for braising. Pull out all the globules of fat from inside the bird around the body cavity opening and from around the neck cavity. Season the inside of the bird lightly with

salt.

Prick the skin with the tines of a fork several places in the fatty areas around the breast and thigh. Chop off the wings at the first joint from the tip and add those pieces to the stock (see below). The bird will keep its shape during cooking if trussed with string (see directions for trussing given in Roast Chicken*).

Brown the duckling. Place it in a heavy casserole in a very hot pre-heated oven. Lay the bird first on one side, then the other and, finally, breast up. Brown for 10 minutes in each position for a total browning time of 30 minutes.

Begin the duck stock. While the duckling is browning in the oven, brown together in a small skillet:

1 Tbs. (15 ml) oil,

the duckling giblets and wing tips,

1 medium carrot, sliced,

½ medium onion, sliced.

Braise the duckling. Remove the casserole from the oven and reduce the heat to 350 F (160 C). Pour out all the fat from the casserole. Place in the casserole around the duck:

> the browned giblets and vegetables,
> 1 cup (250 ml) water.

Add an herb bouquet:

> 3 sprigs parsley,
> 1 stalk celery,
> pinch thyme,
> ⅓ domestic bay leaf.

Deglaze the skillet in which the giblets were browned with

> ½ cup (125 ml) dry white wine.

Stir to scrape up all the browned particles. Add the deglazing wine to the casserole with the duck. Bring the casserole to simmering on top of the stove, cover it, and return it to the oven. Braise for 1 hour, basting twice with the liquid in the casserole. When the duckling is cooked remove it to a hot platter.

Prepare the Orange Sauce. Strain the pan stock from the casserole and skim it quickly, but thoroughly, of fat. Add to the skimmed braising stock:

> ½ cup (125 ml) sauce Espagnole,
> 1 Tbs. (15 ml) beef jelly,
> 2 Tbs. (30 ml) Cognac,
> juice of 1 orange.

Simmer a few moments and add:

> the reserved julienned orange peel,
> salt lightly to taste,
> a grind of pepper (very lightly).

Simmer a few moments longer while arranging the previously prepared orange slices on the platter around the duck. Spoon some of the sauce over the duckling to glaze it and some around it on the platter. Pour the remaining sauce into a sauce dish.

Serve. Carve the duckling at the table in thin slices and accompany each serving with a spoonful or two of Orange Sauce. Risotto* is the best background for the combined flavors of duckling and orange.

Wine Guide. Select a good Chablis, Claret, or a varietal within those groups.

ALTERNATE METHODS FOR PREPARING DUCKLING

(1) *Roasted duckling.* Prepare it for cooking as directed above. Then, following the procedure for Roasted Chicken,* lay the duckling on a bed of vegetables in a roasting pan and roast it for 1 hour and 20-40 minutes

until medium-rare. The juices from the thickest part of the thigh, when pricked, will run yellow with a hint of rose.

(2) *Stock for soups.* Simmer the carcass of roasted duckling in water to cover with vegetables and herbs. See the note after Roasted Chicken.*

(3) *Duckling with sauerkraut.* Use quartered ducklings. Prick the pieces, remove the excess fat, and brown them in oil in a heavy skillet. Add the browned pieces to sauerkraut (see Choucroute Garni*) for the last hour of its cooking.

(4) *Duckling with turnips.* Cook a quartered, browned duckling with peeled, blanched† turnips and onions. Add a bouquet of herbs.† Cook in a heavy casserole, covered, for about 1 hour at 350 F (160 C) or until done. This is the closed casserole roasting method† described for chicken and pork in which no liquid is added during the cooking.

5

Supports for the Framework

The interrelated network of stockmaking, sauces, soufflés, crêpes, batters, and pastry is revealed in this chapter. These extensions enhance the structure of modern French cooking. Here, especially, we see that the old system is sturdy, yet flexible enough to permit renovation. The methods that follow demonstrate traditional devices with certain adjustments and new perspectives. "The old ways" remain consistent with contemporary thinking and requirements and are easily accommodated by our life patterns.

Stockmaking

Using homemade stocks in an overall cooking pattern decidedly improves the general quality of one's cuisine. When used in a sauce or as a braising liquid they lend a special, indefinable depth of flavor. Homemade stocks are recognizably superior to canned stocks.

Stocks, made in quantity, are actually more convenient to use than canned or dehydrated products if they are reduced to "jellies." This is no trouble to accomplish. During the initial simmering, stocks may cook virtually unattended for hours. The entire process to final reduction may span several days, and may be worked comfortably into a busy schedule. Stocks are reduced to jelly form by boiling a large quantity of stock down to a small amount of highly concentrated, gelatinous liquid. When chilled, this liquid sets to a very firm consistency that may be cut into cubes, frozen, and used as needed.

On this basis, stockmaking need only be done two or three times a year and the jelly it yields is very useful. A cube of jelly is easily reconstituted in a cup of water for an "instant" stock. Sometimes jelly is added undiluted to other sauces to achieve an intensified, enriched flavor.

Stock cubes may also be used as a base for soup. Soups, like stocks, are much better when freshly made and having a supply of base on hand

111

encourages their frequent inclusion in a dietary pattern.

Meat jelly cubes are also used with some new techniques for vegetables developed in this book. They convert cooking liquids to a savory stock while by-passing long cooking processes that destroy vegetables' many valuable nutrients.

The value of stockmaking cannot be overstressed. It is this skill, more than any other single factor, that has been lost to us today and makes us dependent on canned and prepackaged products with their heavy-handed seasonings, stripped-down nutrients, and bolstered additive content.

Stockmaking, therefore, is pivotal to good cooking. Its function is fascinating because it is paradoxical. Stock acts as the basis for many sauces, soups, and meat and vegetable dishes; and it also incorporates many valuable elements that would otherwise be thrown away: bones, carcasses, giblets, odd parts, and meat and vegetable trimmings. It is impossible to exclude stockmaking from a comprehensive cooking plan.

CHICKEN STOCK AND JELLY

Ingredients

giblets from 2-4 chickens	celery
odd parts, wings, backs, as available	leeks, if available
	parsnips, optional
collected bones and carcasses	salt
small chicken, if needed	parsley
carrots	thyme
onion	bay leaf
whole clove	

Save the meat *and* vegetable "remnants" for stockmaking by storing them in plastic bags in the freezer. It is possible to make a good stock from collected odds and ends, but adding a small whole chicken insures the stock will have rich flavor and good body.

Cautionary notes. (1) *Do not cover* the stock at any time during cooking or cooling. This causes the stock to sour.

(2) *Do not boil;* the fat and scum will combine to cloud the stock.

Make the stock. Add to an 8 qt. (8 l) kettle and cover with cold water:
giblets from 2–4 chickens and odd parts such as wings, backs,
additional bones, especially a carcass from roasted chicken,
1 small chicken, if needed,
2 medium carrots, scrubbed, quartered,
1 onion stuck with
1 whole clove,
2 leeks, well washed, if available,
1–2 parsnips, optional,
2 tsp. (10 g) salt.

Add a bouquet of herbs:
>2 stalks celery,
>3 sprigs parsley,
>pinch thyme,
>½ domestic bay leaf.

Bring slowly to a low boil, removing the scum (foam) with a slotted spoon as it rises to the top. Reduce the heat and simmer for 2 hours.

Remove the chicken. If a whole chicken was added to the stock pot take it out at this point, bone it, and return the carcass to the simmering stock. The poached meat may be utilized in any recipe requiring previously cooked chicken (see Index). Continue to simmer the stock for 2 to 3 hours longer.

Strain the stock. Pour the stock through a large strainer into a bowl to cool.

Chill the stock. Refrigerate the cooled stock at least overnight. It is still not necessary to cover it because the surface will be protected by the fat that accumulates at the top and forms a seal.

Prepare stock for reduction. Remove all the hardened fat from the surface. Pour off the jellied stock into a saucepan. The sediment in the bottom may be discarded.

Make the jelly. Bring the fat-free stock to a hard boil and continue boiling until the liquid is reduced to about 1½ cups (375 ml). Strain through a fine sieve into a smaller saucepan. Continue to boil the stock until it is reduced to ½–¾ cup (125-180 ml) of thickened syrup. Watch the stock carefully during this final reduction. Pour again through a fine sieve into a small, clean jar.

Final steps. When the liquid is completely cool, cover and refrigerate. When it is set, the jelly may be cut into cubes, placed on a tray, and frozen. After they are hard-frozen, transfer the jelly cubes to a freezer bag for storage. They may be taken out individually as needed.

BROWN BEEF STOCK AND JELLY ▬▬▬▬▬▬▬▬

Ingredients

beef bones	tomatoes, optional
veal bones	celery
carrots	parsley
onion	thyme
salt	bay leaf
peppercorns	stewing beef
leeks, if available	oil
garlic	cheesecloth, optional

Cautionary notes. (1) *Do not cover* the stock at any time during cooking or cooling. This causes the stock to sour.

(2) *Do not boil;* the fat and scum will combine to cloud the stock.

Preheat the oven 450 F (210 C).

Initial browning. Spread out in a roasting pan:

  3 lbs. (1.5 kg) beef bones, cracked,
  1 lb. (450 g) veal bones,
  2 large carrots, scrubbed, quartered,
  1 large onion, peeled, quartered.

Brown in the preheated oven for 30 to 40 minutes until well browned, stirring occasionally.

Add the liquid. Transfer the browned bones and vegetables to a large kettle and pour over them

  5 qt. (5 l) cold water.

Pour the fat out of the roasting pan and add to it

  1½ cups (375 ml) water.

Bring to boiling to deglaze the pan. Scrape up all the browned bits from the bottom and sides. Add the deglazed pan juices to the kettle. Bring the contents of the kettle almost to a boil, skimming off the scum (foam) with a slotted spoon as it rises to the top.

Reduce the heat to simmer.

Season the stock. Add:

  1 Tbs. (15 g) salt,
  4 peppercorns,
  1–2 well-washed leeks, if available,
  1 clove garlic, unpeeled,
  1–2 tomatoes, chopped, optional.

Add a bouquet of herbs:

  2 stalks celery,
  4–6 sprigs parsley,
  pinch thyme,
  ½ domestic bay leaf.

Prepare the meat. Brown together in a skillet:

  1 lb. (450 g) stewing beef,
  1½ Tbs. (20 ml) oil.

Add the browned meat to the stock pot. To facilitate its removal the meat may be tied in a large piece of cheesecloth. Pour any remaining fat from the skillet. Deglaze† it with a little water and add the browning juices to the simmering stock.

Remove the stock meat. After 2 to 3 hours, when the meat is tender, remove it and 1½ cups (375 ml) of the stock and use it in making Beef Hachis.* Or, remove only the beef, without the stock, and utilize it in any of the suggestions for previously cooked beef (see Index). Continue simmering the stock for a total cooking time of about 5 hours.

Make beef jelly. Follow the same procedure described for cooling, chilling, reducing, and storing chicken stock.

Five Indispensable Sauces

The majority of French sauces fall into two broad categories depending on the method by which they are thickened. Generally, sauces are thickened either with a roux or with egg yolks. The class of egg-thickened sauces includes mayonnaise, Hollandaise, and their variations. But, with one exception (a variation of mayonnaise used with a salad), they have not been included in this book.

There are several reasons for this omission. Primarily, these sauces are embellishments and not, therefore, "indispensable." Though delicious, they are very rich and their dietary desirability is thereby limited. Egg yolks boost the cholesterol count of these sauces, and one hardly need mention the great quantities of butter contained in Hollandaise. (To meet modern requirements even egg enrichments have been eliminated from the sauces that follow.) Another drawback is that egg-thickened sauces are much trickier to make. They can enhance a once-a-year fling such as Eggs Benedict on New Year's morning. But, for practical purposes, they fall outside the realm of everyday cooking.

Instead, the emphasis in this volume has been placed on the roux-thickened sauces. They are flexible, adaptable, low in calories, and easy to construct. There are two types. The light sauces are made with milk or light stocks from poultry, fish, or unbrowned veal. The dark, roux-thickened sauces use a rich brown beef stock for the liquid.

The success of these sauces lies in cooking the roux itself. A roux is a mixture of equal parts of butter and flour. It must be sufficiently cooked before any liquid is added to it or the sauce will taste "pasty." If the sauce uses a light liquid, then the roux is cooked to the point that it begins to turn slightly brown in color. Conversely, if the liquid is dark, the roux is cooked to a dark brown color.

Brown sauces accompany dark meats and certain vegetables. The light ones are used for creaming light meats, fish, and vegetables. In different proportions, they make the base for soufflés, croquettes, and crème soups.

An important adaptation of traditional cooking to suit modern needs is developed in the section on pan sauce conversions. Pan sauces are especially useful when homemade stocks and jellies are not available. These new techniques afford a means of short cutting long processes without compromising quality in the result.

The final sauces in this section are not thickened at all, but are simply combined. The tomato sauce is cooked; the vinaigrette is not. Both have wide-ranging applications in enhancing the presentation of meats and vegetables.

Light Roux-Thickened Sauces

BÉCHAMEL SAUCE

Ingredients

    milk
    butter
    flour
    salt and pepper

Select two saucepans: one thin and a heavy one. Pour into the lightweight pan and heat to boiling
    1 cup (250 ml) milk.[1]
Make the roux. Melt in the heavy-bottomed pan over medium-high heat
    2 Tbs. (30 g) butter.
When the butter foams up and begins to subside blend in
    2 Tbs. (30 g) flour.
Cook, stirring, until the mixture is bubbling well and just beginning to color a very pale brown. By this time the milk will be very hot, nearly boiling. Take the butter-flour roux off the heat.
Add the liquid. Pour in the hot milk, stirring with a wire whip. Return the sauce to the heat. Boil, whisking for 1 or 2 minutes until thickened. Season with:
    ¼ tsp. salt,
    1–2 grinds pepper.
Variations. (1) Cream Sauce. Blend in ¼ cup (60 ml) cream and a few drops of lemon juice.
(2) Mornay Sauce. Blend in ¼ cup (60 ml) grated Swiss cheese and a pinch of nutmeg. Thin out with 1–2 Tbs. (15-30 ml) cream.
(3) Curry Sauce. Cook with the butter before adding the flour, 1 Tbs. (15 ml) minced onion. Season the finished sauce with 1–2 tsp. curry powder to suit taste. Thin if necessary with 1–2 Tbs. (15-30 ml) cream.
(4) Paprika Sauce. Follow the directions for curry sauce substituting paprika for curry powder.
(5) Mushroom Sauce. Add to the finished sauce 1–2 Tbs. (15-30 ml) mushroom duxelles.*
(6) Velouté Sauce. Substitute chicken stock or fish cooking liquid for milk. An example of a velouté sauce for fish is given in Poached Salmon.* A thickened version of velouté sauce made with chicken stock serves as the base for crème soups.

---

[1] For special diets, skim milk and margarine may be substituted in the béchamel sauce without significantly altering the quality of the sauce.

Dark Roux-Thickened Sauces

SAUCE ESPAGNOLE ▐███████████████████████████████▌

Ingredients

brown beef stock*	flour
carrot	tomato paste
celery	parsley
onion	bay leaf
boiled ham	thyme
oil	salt and pepper

This brown sauce requires long, slow cooking to develop a really rich flavor, but it is not difficult to make. It is helpful to prepare enough to last awhile and freeze it in several half-pint (250 ml) jars until needed.

Heat the liquid. Bring slowly to boiling in a large saucepan
     6 cups (1.5 l) brown beef stock.

Prepare the vegetables. Cook together slowly for about 10 minutes in a heavy, 2 qt. (2 l) saucepan:
     1 carrot, minced,
     1 stalk celery, minced,
     1 medium onion, minced,
     1 thin slice boiled ham, minced,
     ½ cup (125 ml) cooking oil.

Make the roux. Add to the cooked vegetables
     ½ cup (125 ml) flour.

Cook, stirring, over low to moderate heat until the flour is a rich brown (about 8 to 10 minutes). Remove the roux from the heat.

Add the liquid. Pour in the boiling stock, whisking to smooth, and blend in
     2 Tbs. (30 ml) tomato paste.

Add a bouquet of herbs:
     3 sprigs parsley,
     ¼ domestic bay leaf,
     pinch thyme.

Partly cover and cook the sauce very slowly for about 2 hours, skimming and stirring it now and then. Taste for seasoning, adding if necessary
     salt and pepper.

Strain the sauce, cool uncovered, and store.

Variations. Many sauces derived from sauce Espagnole are presented in Chapter 4:
    (1) Sauce Parisienne,*
    (2) Sauce Diable,*
    (3) Madeira Sauce,*
    (4) Bordelaise Sauce.*

Pan Sauce Conversions

VERSION I. STOCK CONVERSION

Never discard the pan sauces that result from deglazing† pans in which meats have been roasted† or sautéed.† Braising liquid used in covered casserole cooking of beef, chicken, and veal is also valuable and should never be discarded. These may substitute for stock in making a Velouté or a quick version of sauce Espagnole.

They may be stored for several days in the refrigerator and, if there is not an immediate use for them, they may be labeled and frozen. Once refrigerated they acquire a dense, gelatinous consistency. Any fat content separates out and settles on top and may, therefore, be easily removed before reusing.

The flavor of these pan sauces is quite concentrated and so they may usually be diluted and extended with the addition of a little water or wine. When only a small amount of sauce is required to accompany a dish, it is a great convenience to utilize these liquids for that purpose. For instance, half a cup of braising liquid plus a little water or wine may be thickened with a roux† of 1 Tbs. each (15 g each) of butter and flour. One or two spoonfuls of cream may be added if it is appropriate to the dish. Though the original sauce will probably have been seasoned with a basic herb bouquet†, its character can be changed with the addition of a tiny pinch of another herb. Other seasonings such as sautéed mushrooms, mushroom duxelles,* or capers may be stirred in just before serving.

VERSION II. JELLY CONVERSION

These remarkable pan sauce liquids have another useful function. One or two spoonfuls of a richly concentrated sauce may substitute for a meat jelly* in other sauces. For example, sauté lamb chops in a heavy skillet. When the chops are done remove them to a hot plate and pour out all the fat from the pan. Deglaze† the pan with ¾ cup (180 ml) tomato sauce* and 1–2 Tbs. (15-30 ml) white or red wine, and stir in 1 or 2 spoonfuls concentrated pan sauce or braising liquid from a beef roast. The use of this technique can make a crucial difference. It adds great depth and an indefinable, "secret" flavor to insure the success of a dish.

VINAIGRETTE SAUCE ▮▮▮▮▮▮▮▮▮▮▮▮▮▮▮▮▮▮▮▮▮▮▮▮▮▮▮

Ingredients

wine vinegar	Dijon mustard
oil	parsley
salt and pepper	other fresh herbs, if available

Combine the components. Measure into a jar with a tight-fitting lid and shake well to blend:

>2 tsp. wine vinegar,
>2 Tbs. (30 ml) oil,
>dash salt,
>1–2 grinds pepper,
>¼ tsp. Dijon mustard,
>1 sprig parsley, minced,
>other fresh herbs, if available.

Variations. (1) Vinaigrette with Cream. Substitute lemon juice for wine vinegar. Add 2 Tbs. (30 ml) cream and a pinch of dill. This may be used as a sauce for fish.

(2) Dijon Mustard Sauce. Mash together:

>¼ tsp. salt,
>⅓ clove garlic or 1 shallot, minced.

Blend in:

>2 Tbs. (30 ml) Dijon mustard,
>juice of ¼ lemon,
>1–2 grinds pepper,
>2 sprigs parsley, minced,
>pinch thyme, optional.

Add slowly, beating with a fork

>3 Tbs. (45 ml) oil.

Use as a sauce for coating broiled meats and as a dip for vegetables such as steamed artichokes.

(3) A Mayonnaise-like Sauce. A version using the ingredients for vinaigrette with the addition of hard-boiled egg yolks appears in Veal Salad, Parisian Style.*

(4) Lemon Juice Marinade. A variation of vinaigrette used as a marinade is given in Lamb Shish Kebab.*

TOMATO SAUCE

Ingredients

butter	tomatoes	parsley
oil	salt and pepper	celery
onion	sugar	thyme
garlic	tomato paste	bay leaf
carrot	meat jelly* or pan sauce†	

Prepare the vegetables. Cook together slowly in a small skillet for 5 minutes:

>½ Tbs. (8 ml) each of butter and oil,
>½ medium onion,
>1 large clove garlic, crushed, peeled,
>½ medium carrot, minced.

Then add
 3 medium tomatoes, chopped.
Cover the pan and continue cooking for 10 minutes.
Season the sauce. When the tomatoes have rendered their juices add:
 salt and pepper, lightly to taste,
 pinch sugar,
 1 Tbs. (15 ml) tomato paste,
 1 Tbs. (15 ml) meat jelly or pan sauce.
Add a bouquet of herbs:
 3 sprigs parsley,
 1 small stalk celery,
 pinch thyme,
 ¼ domestic bay leaf.
Simmer partially covered for 20-30 minutes.
Purée the sauce. Rub the sauce through a sieve using a wooden spoon. This removes the tomato skins and other extraneous fibers and gives a good texture to the sauce. Or, process the sauce through a food mill.

Variation. Mediterranean-Flavored Tomato Sauce. Add to the seasonings in the basic recipe:
 ¼ tsp. fennel seeds,
 ½ tsp. basil,
 ¼x¼x2 inch (.5x.5x5 cm) piece of orange peel

Soufflés and Crêpes

French invention and thrift have produced two of the most valuable devices in a cooking repertoire. The chef's trick with leftovers is to transform them into something elegant and for this he often relies on crêpes and soufflés. Significantly, they are both created from ingredients in common use and always at hand: eggs, milk, flour, and butter. Although variations of the crêpes principle appear around the world, none duplicates the French crêpe for lightness and flavor.

The soufflé, on the other hand, is uniquely French. Reputedly difficult to make, the mystery vanishes once one learns the soufflé's component parts and assembly procedure. Step-by-step directions are given which will eliminate confusion and produce a perfect soufflé every time. Crêpe construction is outlined in a similar manner. A guide for baking and filling crêpes in a continuous process along with several suggestions for their final presentation conclude this section.

THE SOUFFLÉ

Ingredients

butter	eggs
flour	flavor ingredient
milk	

The basic soufflé consists of three parts: (1) the base (a thick béchamel); (2) flavor ingredient (minced meat, vegetable, or cheese); (3) eggs (yolks enrich the base, whites lighten the mixture). Prepare and assemble the soufflé following the procedure outlined below.

Prepare the soufflé dish. Butter the bottom and sides of a soufflé dish, charlotte mold, or 1½ qt. (1.5 l) casserole. Coat with
> fine dry bread crumbs.

Preheat the oven 400 F (185 C). Place the rack on the middle level.

Prepare the flavor ingredient. Measure
> 1 cup (250 ml) meat, fish, vegetables or cheese, minced, puréed, grated, or finely diced.

Make the base. In a saucepan cook a béchamel sauce* in the following proportions:
> 3 Tbs. (45 g) butter,
> 3 Tbs. (45 g) flour,
> 1¼ cups (300 ml) milk.

Cook until reduced to 1 cup (250 ml).

Add the flavor ingredient. Fold the meat, vegetables, or cheese into the base. Cook-stir over low heat to blend; remove the pan from the heat.

Separate the eggs. Place in a 2 qt. (2 l) bowl
> 5 egg whites.

Add the yolks to the base. Beat in, one at a time
> 4 egg yolks.

The fifth yolk may be discarded or kept refrigerated and added to cream sauce* or scrambled eggs.

Return the sauce base to the heat. Cook a moment longer on low heat so that the eggs will bind the mixture. Remove the saucepan from the heat again.

Beat the egg whites. With an electric mixer beat the whites until they are stiff, but not dry.

Add the egg whites to the base. Fold into the base mixture by fourths. Blend in the first addition (¼ of the stiffly-beaten egg whites) very well with a wire whip to lighten the entire mixture. Fold in the remaining fourths in separate additions, taking great care not to break them down. Blend as little as possible, folding just enough to combine the egg whites with the base.

Bake the soufflé. Turn the soufflé into the prepared pan; set in the preheated oven. Immediately turn the temperature down to 375 F (170 C). Bake 25 to 30 minutes. Serve at once.

CRÊPES

Ingredients

milk	flour	béchamel sauce or variation*
cold water	salt	cooked meat or shellfish
sugar	butter	cooked vegetables, optional
eggs	Cognac	

Make the batter in advance. This is an all-purpose batter which may be used for either main dish or dessert crêpes. Combine in a large bowl:

¾ cup (180 ml) milk,
¾ cup (180 ml) cold water,
1 Tbs. (15 g) sugar.

Beat in one at a time
4 eggs.

Add, a little at a time, blending with a wire whip until smooth:
1½ cups (6 oz. or 170 g) sifted flour,
pinch salt.

Pour over and blend well
2 Tbs. (30 ml) melted butter.

To remove any lumps pour the batter through a strainer into another bowl. Refrigerate for several hours or overnight. Just before making the crêpes beat into the batter
2 Tbs. (30 ml) Cognac.

Assemble the filling. Fillings for crêpes usually consist of:
cooked shellfish, or
cooked poultry, diced and/or
cooked vegetables, sliced or diced.

Fold meat/vegetables into
béchamel sauce or one of its variations.

Double the amounts in the sauce recipe. Combine half with the filling ingredients; use the remainder to cover the completed crêpes.

Bake the crêpes. Consider the first crêpe in the pan a trial run. It seldom browns well and often tears on turning. After the first one you will have established the temperature and technique. Heat a heavy pan or griddle until a drop of water skitters over the surface. Take the pan from the heat and quickly skim the end of a stick of butter over the pan to film the bottom lightly. Return the pan to the heat. Pour a scant ¼ cup (60 ml) of the batter into the middle of the griddle. Wait a second or two, then tip and roll the pan so that the batter spreads into a 6 to 8-inch (15-20 cm) circle. Cook over medium heat until the bottom of the crêpe is a golden brown color.

Turn the crêpe. Using a spatula, carefully lift the side of the crêpe that is nearest you. Pull it up and over to cook on the other side for a moment.

Transfer the crêpe. Invert the griddle over a plate so that the crêpe falls onto the plate with the brown side down and the pale side up. This way, the crêpe will be in position to be filled; when rolled, the browned side will show. Repeat the process until the desired number of crêpes has been made or until all the batter has been used.

Blanket the crêpes. Cover the filled and rolled crêpes with more of the sauce (without the filling ingredient) to protect them during reheating from drying out.

Final preparations. Sprinkle over the filled, sauced crêpes:
    grated Swiss cheese,
    pieces of butter over the top.
Final heating. At this point a dish of crêpes may be glazed under the broiler and served immediately. Otherwise, the crêpes may wait an hour or may be covered and refrigerated for several hours. Reheat 30 minutes before serving time in the upper level of a preheated 375 F (170 C) oven.

ALTERNATE PROCEDURE

To bake and fill crêpes in a continuous effort follow this pattern:

(1) While the heavy griddle is heating, butter the baking dish which is to receive the crêpes and assemble all utensils conveniently: (a) the crêpe filling in a bowl along with a knife for spreading; (b) a plate to hold a ¼ cup (60 ml) measure and a stick of butter; (c) another plate to receive the crêpe for rolling.

(2) Bake 1 crêpe and transfer it to the plate for rolling, pale side up.

(3) With the skillet removed from the heat, rapidly make 3 or 4 sweeps with the butter stick over the surface of the pan.

(4) Return the skillet to the fire to reheat briefly.

(5) Pour ¼ cup (60 ml) batter into the center of the pan.

(6) Refill the measure and set it on the plate.

(7) Tip and roll the skillet to spread the batter into a 6 to 8-inch (15-20 cm) circle.

(8) While the crêpe is baking on the first side, quickly spread the previously made crêpe with filling.

(9) Turn the crêpe that is baking in the pan.

(10) Pull the griddle off the heat. The underside of the crêpe will cook from the heat retained in the pan.

(11) Roll the previously baked and filled crêpe and transfer it to the buttered baking dish.

(12) Turn the crêpe from the griddle out onto the rolling plate. Return the griddle to the heat and repeat this process from step 3. Continue until the desired number of crêpes has been made or until all the batter has been used.

SERVING SUGGESTIONS FOR CRÊPES

(1) *Folded crêpes.* Instead of rolling crêpes around the filling, simply fold in half with a generous spoonful of filling inside.

(2) *Stacked crêpes.* Another convenient and attractive method does not require rolling or folding. Place a baked crêpe flat in a buttered baking dish and spread the filling over it. Repeat this process until a torte-like mound or stack of crêpes has been built. In this presentation two complementary fillings may be used on alternate layers: mushroom-spinach, ham-cheese, chicken-broccoli. Cover the stacked crêpes with sauce,

cheese, and butter. Reheat half an hour in the oven before serving. Cut in wedges to serve.

(3) *Hors d'oeuvre.* Bake half-size crêpes using 2 Tbs. (30 ml) batter; fill and roll.

Frying Batter and Pastry

These devices are especially useful in transforming previously cooked meats and vegetables into interesting secondary dishes. Batter and pastry are good insulators against high heat. Each of these is an all-purpose recipe that may be used for any part of the meal from entrée to dessert.

FRYING BATTER

Ingredients

flour	Cognac
salt	beer
sugar	lukewarm water
oil	egg

If this batter is to be made long in advance it may be refrigerated, but it must be allowed to return to room temperature before using.

Combine the batter. Mix in a bowl in the order given:
1 cup (4 oz. or 112 g) sifted flour,
¼ tsp. salt,
¼ tsp. sugar,
1 Tbs. (15 ml) oil,
1 Tbs. (15 ml) Cognac,
2 Tbs. (30 ml) beer,
¾ cup (180 ml) lukewarm water.

Blend with a wire whip until smooth and free from lumps. Cover with a damp towel and allow to ferment at room temperature for 2 hours.

Final step. Just before using, beat in
1 egg.

PROCEDURE FOR DEEP-FRYING

(1) Batter and foods to be fried should be at room temperature.

(2) Add the fat to a heavy, deep-sided pan such as a cast-iron Dutch oven. The fat may be a vegetable shortening or cooking oil or a combination of the two, but it must be sufficiently deep for foods to float.

(3) Heat the fat to very hot, almost smoking.

(4) Dip foods in the batter and add to the fat a few at a time.

(5) Foods brown on the side that is closest to the heat source. Turn during cooking to brown evenly.

(6) When the batter coating is golden, remove with a slotted spoon onto brown paper to drain. Serve at once.

(7) After the fat has cooled, strain the cooking fat through a sieve into a covered container. Store in the refrigerator. It may be used a number of times before discarding. Fat may be "cleansed" of flavors from previous use by first cooking a sliced potato in it.

SERVING SUGGESTIONS FOR DEEP-FRIED FOODS

(1) *Cheese fritters.* Cut Swiss cheese into thin slices; dip in batter and fry in very hot fat.

(2) *Fish and shellfish.* Wash fish in cider vinegar and rinse quickly and thoroughly under running cold water. Or, marinate the fish in salt and lemon juice for 30 minutes. Wash off the marinade and dry the fish. Dip serving-sized portions of fish in the batter and fry until the batter is nicely browned.

(3) *Apple fritters.* Peel and core about 4 apples. Cut in crosswise slices making rings. Dip in batter and fry. Remove from the fat. Drain on brown paper and sprinkle with sugar.

(4) *Banana fritters.* Peel bananas and cut in 2 pieces. Dip in the batter and fry. Drain on brown paper and sprinkle with powdered sugar.

PASTRY

Ingredients

butter	flour
lard	ice water
salt	egg

Egg gives this dough sufficient body to shape it over the outside of cake pans and muffin tins, making it possible to bake freestanding shells for tarts and tartlets without springform pans. Lard is used for flakiness, the butter for flavor.

Mix the pastry. Cut together and blend with a pastry blender:

5 Tbs. (2½ oz. or 75 g) butter, firmly chilled,
5 Tbs. (2½ oz. or 75 g) lard, firmly chilled,
¼ tsp. salt,
2 cups (8 oz. or 225 g) sifted flour.

Combine and pour over, blending rapidly with 2–3 sweeping stirs with a large fork:

5 Tbs. (75 ml) ice water,
1 Tbs. (15 ml) beaten egg.

Add, if necessary

1 additional Tbs. (15 ml) ice water.

Collect all the pieces together. Blend slightly with 3 or 4 kneading motions. Shape quickly into a smooth, flattened mass. Wrap in waxed paper and chill 2 hours or more before rolling.

Preheat the oven 425 F (200 C).

Roll out the pastry. Always roll the pin over the pastry dough by starting close to you and rolling away. After each roll lift the pastry with a hand under each side and turn the round of pastry clockwise one quarter turn. Make certain there is always sufficient flour on the board to prevent sticking. Roll the pastry out to an even ⅛-inch (3 cm) thickness.

Shape the pastry. Carefully lift the dough and place it in or over buttered pans. Trim the pastry even with the outside lip of the pan and fold the cut edge under. You may mark the folded edge of the pastry in a decorative pattern, if you wish, using the handle of a fork to make an impression in the dough. Prick the walls and bottom very well with the tines of a fork.

Support the pastry. This pastry is very rich and if it is to be baked unfilled the sides must be supported so they will not collapse as the butter melts with the heat of the oven. After lining the pan and pricking the pastry, fit a sheet of aluminum foil on top of the pastry and fill the pan with dried beans. Leave the edges of foil free so that foil and beans may be easily lifted out together from the pastry.

Bake the pastry. Place the pan on the middle level of the preheated oven. If, as in making a quiche, a filling is to be added later to finish baking with the crust, bake the pastry until partially done (just beginning to brown lightly), about 7 minutes. A fully cooked pastry is finished to a golden brown in about 12 minutes. (A beans and foil support may be removed after about 8 minutes to allow the pastry to brown well. At this point the sides are sufficiently strong and they will not fall.)

6

Vegetables and Grains

Contemporary cooking is concerned not only with extending meats, it also strives to preserve the nutritional content of vegetables. For this reason, special attention has been given to their preparation in this volume. With these concerns in mind, several new techniques have been developed for vegetable cookery.

The standard French method for cooking green vegetables is to boil them in a large quantity of water and cook rapidly until they are just tender. By comparison, the steaming method outlined in this chapter produces equally satisfactory results and overcomes nutritionists' valid objection that vitamin content is largely lost in cooking by the old method. In this particular approach to steaming, the traditional use of beurre maniét as a thickening agent is employed to transform the cooking liquid into a sauce.

Actually, two methods have been developed for steaming vegetables and both combine values of the old with the new. Method A is for vegetables that do not require peeling. However, many vegetables must be peeled in order to cook evenly and be truly palatable. This practice of peeling is another point on which nutrition experts take issue with traditional French techniques. Method B is designed to bolster the vitamin content of these vegetables while preserving French standards of preparation.

Steaming is just one approach to vegetable cookery. Many other vegetables are braised, sautéed, or baked, while another new method, called steambaking, revolutionizes potato preparation. With one exception, this chapter emphasizes the preparation of fresh vegetables, preferred for their quality, control over preparation, and higher nutritional content. For every vegetable, the most effective initial cooking method is given. Wherever possible, suggestions are added for varying the vegetable's final presentation.

In keeping with our food utilization theme, a chart follows outlining principles of stuffing vegetables which maximize efficient food use. While some chefs have specific procedures for stuffed vegetables, these dishes should not be thought of as fixed or absolute. Take these opportunities to unleash your imagination and utilize combinations of whatever may be available at the moment.

Until recently, vegetable preparation has been overshadowed by other aspects of American cooking. But a new dietary trend, especially among younger people, is a growing interest in vegetarianism. It is exciting to discover that vegetables can be as challenging to prepare and as varied in their presentation as any other food. The following recipes should give a sense of the potential in this half of the culinary spectrum.

Vegetables

METHOD A

Steaming apparatus can be assembled from the equipment listed in Chapter 2. A splatter screen is suggested to support vegetables over hot water, but, of course, a folding steamer basket may also be used. Most vegetables are cooked in a shallow, covered casserole, but a deeper, oval roaster is used for artichokes. Although lighter weight pans may be substituted, water evaporation will be a critical problem. The water level must be checked and replenished as necessary.

When using the recommended equipment, the vegetables, because they fit closely under the lid, cook quickly and evenly by steam rising from below and falling back as condensation. The liquid in the pan reduces to the correct amount for a sauce. They must be watched so that they do not overcook. Most vegetables require 10 to 15 minutes cooking (or less) but the time will vary somewhat according to the amount, size, and texture of the vegetable being cooked, the type of apparatus used, and the intensity of the heat source.

Recommended vegetables. Use this method for cooking green beans, Brussels sprouts, cabbage, peppers, mushrooms, and other vegetables that do not require peeling.

Prepare the vegetable. Wash, cut into serving-size pieces, or follow the directions given in the specific recipe.

Assemble the steamer. Place in the casserole bottom
     1½ cups (375 ml) water.

Adjust the rack or "shelf" (consult the Equipment List in Chapter 2 for details). Arrange the vegetables prepared for cooking on the shelf in an even layer.

Cook the vegetables. Set the heat at medium-high. When steam begins to rise reduce the heat to medium and secure the lid. Steam the vegetables only until done (just tender through, but bright green in color), about 10-15 minutes. Remove the vegetables at once and plunge them into a large bowl of cold water to stop their cooking.

Convert the cooking liquid to a sauce. Stir into the hot liquid
     1 tsp. (5 g) each of butter and
     flour, mashed together.

Cook until lightly thickened and slightly reduced. Additional butter may be added if desired and, if it would enhance the flavor of the dish, also blend in

    ½ tsp. beef or chicken jelly* (optional).

Season to taste with

    salt and pepper.

In informal, daily cooking the steaming liquid may also be boiled to reduce to about ¼ cup (60 ml) and blended into béchamel sauces.* If it is not incorporated into a sauce, the cooking liquid may be reserved for use in soups.

Serve. Drain the vegetable well and reheat it in the sauce the last minute before serving.

METHOD B

Recommended vegetables. This method is for cooking vegetables that require peeling such as asparagus, broccoli, and cauliflower.

Prepare the vegetable. Proceed according to the directions in the recipe, reserving the peelings.

Assemble the steamer. Follow the same procedure outlined in Method A but spread the peelings over the bottom of the casserole when adding the water, then add the rack of vegetables.

Steam the vegetable. Follow the guidelines given for Method A. When the vegetable is done, remove it to cold water and skim the peelings from the cooking liquid.

Complete the sauce. Follow the suggestions given for Method A.

GREEN BEANS

Green beans go well with most meats—lamb, pork, ham, beef, and veal—or serve them with poultry or firm-fleshed fish such as tuna and halibut. They may accompany the main dish or be served separately.

Prepare the beans for cooking. Snap off the tip from each end of the bean and pull away the "string" that runs down each side. (Some varieties of beans have little string, if any.) Leave the beans whole for steaming and chop them, if desired, after cooking.

Steam the beans. Use Method A and cook the green beans until they are just tender but still bright green.

Convert the cooking liquid to a sauce. Use the outline in the cooking method. Beef or chicken jelly* may be added to the cooking liquid.

SERVING SUGGESTIONS

(1) *Au beurre.* Reheat in plain or lemon-flavored butter.

(2) *Sauced.* Reheat beans in a béchamel,* Mornay,* mushroom,* cream* or tomato sauce.*

(3) *With vegetables.* Add ½ tsp. meat jelly* to the thickened cooking liquid and combine beans with any of the following: small, braised on-

ions*; sautéed mushrooms*; peeled and seeded tomatoes; or diced, steambaked potatoes.* Garnish with chopped parsley.

(4) *Chilled.* Serve with vinaigrette sauce.* Rings of mild red onion may also be included.

Brussels Sprouts

Serve Brussels sprouts with poultry, veal, pork, and ham.

Prepare for cooking. Wash Brussels sprouts well. Cut them lengthwise in half if they are small, in quarters if large.

Steam Brussels sprouts. Use Method A and steam them until they are tender when pierced with a knife but still bright green.

Convert the cooking liquid to a sauce. Use the directions in the cooking method. Chicken jelly* (½ tsp.) may be added to the liquid or a few spoonfuls of cream may be blended in.

Serving Suggestions

(1) *Au beurre.* Reheat Brussels sprouts in plain or lemon-flavored butter.

(2) *Sauced.* Reheat in béchamel,* Mornay,* or cream sauce.*

(3) *Milanese style.* Arrange Brussels sprouts in an ovenproof dish with grated Swiss cheese to cover and melted butter poured over all. Reheat in 450 F (210 C) oven for 5 minutes until the cheese melts.

Asparagus

Asparagus is especially good with chicken, veal, and shellfish and may accompany most other meats as well. If it is served as a course by itself, allow ½ lb. (225 g) per person for a generous serving.

Prepare for cooking. Hold the asparagus stalk in both hands and bend. It will snap and break, separating the tough lower portion from the tender upper stalk. Break each stalk in this manner but do not discard the lower portion. Peel each upper stalk to within 1½ inches (3-4 cm) of the tip, reserving the peelings. Cut the stems to an equal length.

Steam the asparagus. Use Method B, placing both the peelings and lower stalks in the casserole bottom. Asparagus, properly cooked, is tender when pierced with a knife, but not limp.

Convert the cooking liquid to a sauce. Use a beurre manié† adding, if desired, ½ tsp. chicken jelly* or 1–2 Tbs. (15-30 ml) cream. However, the cooking liquid with peelings removed and with the lower stalks peeled and puréed or finely diced could be the basis for an excellent crème soup.*

Serving Suggestions

(1) *Chilled.* Serve with vinaigrette sauce.*

(2) *Au beurre.* Reheat in plain or lemon-flavored butter.

(3) *Sauced.* Reheat in cream* or Mornay* sauce.

(4) *Flemish style.* Reheat in butter and garnish with finely chopped hard-boiled egg.

(5) *Milanese style.* Arrange asparagus in an ovenproof dish and cover with grated cheese and melted butter. Reheat 5 minutes in a 450 F (210 C) oven to melt the cheese.

BROCCOLI

Traditionally, broccoli is associated with Italian cuisine rather than French, but it goes well with meats, poultry, and many kinds of fish.

Prepare broccoli for cooking. Wash it well and remove the leaves. Sever the tops from the "branches" and central stalks and reserve the peelings. Cut the stalks into bite-size pieces.

Steam the broccoli. Use Method B and cook until just tender and bright green.

Convert the cooking liquid to a sauce. Follow the directions in the cooking method. Chicken jelly* may be melted into the sauce.

SERVING SUGGESTIONS

(1) *Au beurre.* Reheat in plain or lemon-flavored butter.

(2) *Sauced.* Reheat in béchamel,* Mornay,* or cream sauce.*

(3) *Milanese style.* Cover with grated Swiss cheese and melted butter and reheat 5 minutes in a 450 F (210 C) oven to melt the cheese.

(4) *Chilled.* Serve chilled broccoli with vinaigrette sauce.* Quartered tomatoes and/or rings of sliced mild red onions may also be included. Rendered, crumbled bacon is a suitable garnish.

CAULIFLOWER

Cauliflower is compatible with lamb, beef, veal, pork, and poultry.

Prepare for cooking. Wash the cauliflower well and cut the flowerets from the central stalk. Separate them into pieces as nearly equal as possible. Peel the stems of the flowerets and add the peelings to the bottom of the steamer. Peel the central stalk, but discard its peelings. Holding a large knife on a slant angle cut the stalk into about 8 diagonal slices.

Steam the cauliflower. Use Method B and cook until it is tender when pierced with a knife.

Convert the cooking liquid to a sauce. Thicken with a beurre manié†. Chicken jelly* may be stirred into the sauce. The stalk and the cooking liquid may be used instead in crème soup.* Save a few flowerets for a garnish.

SERVING SUGGESTIONS

(1) *Au beurre.* Reheat in plain or lemon-flavored butter.

(2) *Sauced.* Reheat in béchamel,* Mornay,* cream,* or curry sauce.*

(3) *Milanese style.* Reheat in the oven with grated Swiss cheese as described above for asparagus and broccoli. Tomatoes—peeled, seeded, juiced, and chopped—may be combined with cauliflower for this variation. Dry bread crumbs may be blended with the cheese topping.

(4) *Polonaise.* Lightly brown ⅓ cup (80 ml) fresh bread crumbs with ½ stick (¼ cup or 60 ml) melted butter and spread over the cauliflower. Garnish with finely chopped hard-boiled egg and chopped parsley.

(5) *Chilled.* Serve cooled cauliflower combined with other cooked, chilled vegetables. Toss lightly with vinaigrette sauce.*

WHOLE STEAMED ARTICHOKES ▬▬▬▬▬▬▬▬▬▬▬▬▬▬▬▬

Artichokes may be served as a separate course and are compatible with beef, veal, lamb, chicken, and shellfish. There is something lost and something gained by steaming artichokes instead of boiling them. The color is not as deeply green, but the artichoke is more tender and flavorful.

Assemble the steamer. A deep-sided oval roaster is the best container for steaming artichokes and, if they are not too large, it will hold four of them. See the Equipment List in Chapter 2 for details. Add to the bottom of the roaster:

1½ cups (375 ml) water,
juice of ½ lemon.

Prepare artichokes for steaming. Break off the stems from the bottom of the artichoke. This pulls out any coarse fibers that extend from the stem into the base. Add the stems to the bottom of the roaster. They may be cooked, sliced, or diced and marinated in vinaigrette sauce* for use in salads. With a knife, trim the stems off evenly at the base of the artichoke. Lay the artichoke on its side on a cutting board. Cut off the top third of the artichoke. With a scissors cut off the prickly tip of each of the remaining outer leaves. Rub all the cut surfaces with lemon juice. For even cooking cut a deep "X" in the base of the artichoke where the stem was removed.

Steam the artichokes. Place them on a rack in the steaming device. Set the heat on medium and when the steam has begun to rise, cover the roaster. Cook until a leaf may be easily removed from the artichoke, about 20 minutes.

Prepare for serving. First, remove the choke. Spread open the leaves and pull out the central mound of tightly closed, purple leaves. With a sharp, thin-edged spoon, carefully scoop out the hairy choke. It comes away cleanly if you scrape deeply enough to take just a little of the base, too. Sprinkle salt and pepper lightly on the base. Replace the central leaves and press the outer leaves together to close the artichoke again.

Serve. Artichokes should be served cool, but not cold. Accompany each artichoke with melted, lemon-flavored butter for dipping the leaves. Or, accompany with vinaigrette sauce* or the Dijon mustard sauce variation.*

Braised Vegetables

Braised Artichokes, Provençal Style

Ingredients

artichokes	salt and pepper
oil	sugar
brown beef or chicken stock*	parsley
onions	thyme
tomatoes	bay leaf
garlic	

Serve as a separate course or with roast beef, lamb, pork, veal, or chicken.

Preheat the oven 350 F (160 C).

Prepare vegetables for cooking. Following the preceding recipe for steamed artichokes, prepare

4 large artichokes,

removing stems and trimming tops and leaf tips. In addition, cut each artichoke into lengthwise quarters and scrape out the choke from each piece. Wash them well and put the sectioned artichokes in a heavy casserole with:

⅓ cup (80 ml) oil,

⅔ cup (160 ml) beef or chicken stock,

8 small white onions, peeled,

1 large clove garlic, crushed,

2 medium tomatoes, peeled, seeded, quartered,

pinch each of salt and sugar,

2–3 grinds pepper.

Add a bouquet of herbs:

3 sprigs parsley,

pinch thyme,

¼ domestic bay leaf.

Cook the casserole. Bring the contents to simmering on top of the stove. Cover the casserole and place it in the preheated oven. Bake for 1 hour until the artichokes are tender and the liquid is reduced. Baste the vegetables 1 or 2 times during their cooking.

Serve. Garnish with chopped parsley.

Braised Celery

Ingredients

celery	carrot
butter	brown beef stock*
onion	sauce Espagnole*

Serve braised celery as a separate course, with bread to take up the sauce.

Prepare the vegetables for cooking. Wash thoroughly and cut off the leaves from

8 stalks of celery.

Cut each stalk into 4 pieces. Bring to boiling

1 qt. (1 l) water.

Drop the celery into the water. Turn off the heat and let the celery set in the water for 5 minutes while sautéing in a small skillet:

½ Tbs. (8 g) butter,
1 small onion, sliced,
1 medium carrot, sliced.

Lift the celery out of the water with a slotted spoon and transfer it to the skillet. Place the celery over the carrot and onion. Pour in to half cover the vegetables

beef stock.

Cook the celery. Heat to simmering; cover the skillet, and cook very slowly for 20 to 30 minutes without overcooking. Lift out the vegetables and arrange on serving dishes. Add to the cooking liquid in the skillet

½–⅔ cup (125-160 ml) sauce Espagnole.

Boil down the sauce very rapidly until it is nicely thickened. Pour the hot sauce over the vegetables and serve at once.

SPINACH ████████████████████████████████████

Ingredients

spinach	butter
salt and pepper	flour

This vegetable is very flexible and may be served with nearly any meat, poultry, and broiled or sautéed fish.

Prepare spinach for cooking. During cooking, spinach reduces its volume considerably. For each 4 persons prepare

2 lbs. (1 kg) spinach.

It must be thoroughly washed. Plunge the whole bunches into 2 or 3 changes of water. Then, wash each leaf under running water and remove its stem. Place the leaves as you wash them in a large stainless steel saucepan or enamel kettle.

Cook the spinach. Use no more water than that which clings to the leaves from washing. Sprinkle the spinach lightly with

salt and pepper.

Cover the kettle and cook down over medium heat for about 5 minutes. Lift the lid several times and stir to lift the cooked leaves from the bottom. Once all the leaves have "wilted," remove the spinach to a strainer placed over a bowl. Press the vegetable mass with a wooden spoon to eliminate as much liquid as possible. Place the spinach on a cutting board and chop it into bite-size pieces.

Convert the cooking liquid to a sauce. Cook in a small skillet until just starting to brown a roux of:

> 1 Tbs. (15 g) butter,
> 1 Tbs. (15 g) flour.

Blend in, whisking to smooth
> the spinach cooking liquid.

Add the chopped spinach to the skillet and simmer 2 or 3 minutes longer over low heat.

SERVING SUGGESTIONS

(1) *Lyonnaise.* Minced shallots or onions may be cooked with the butter before adding the flour to make the roux.†

(2) *Spinach braised in stock.* Add a small piece of beef or chicken jelly* to the cooking liquid before adding it to the roux.

(3) *Creamed spinach.* Stir 2 or 3 Tbs. (15-30 ml) cream into the sauce and a small pinch of nutmeg before the final reheating.

(4) *Garni.* Arrange slices of hard-boiled egg over cooked spinach.

(5) *Other seasonings:* grated Swiss cheese and/or sautéed, minced mushrooms may be added to any of the above suggestions.

SIMMERED MUSHROOMS ▬▬▬▬▬▬▬▬▬▬▬

Ingredients

> mushrooms
> butter
> salt
> water or chicken stock*
> fresh lemon juice

Mushrooms cooked this way will retain their light color and blend well with delicate dishes.

Prepare mushrooms for cooking. Select only fresh mushrooms with caps tightly closed to the stem. Wash each carefully and slice

> ½ lb. (225 g) mushrooms.

Combine in a saucepan with:

> 1 Tbs. (15 g) butter,
> ⅛ tsp. salt,
> 2 Tbs. (30 ml) water or chicken stock,
> juice of ¼ lemon.

Cover and simmer 3 to 5 minutes.

PEAS ██

Ingredients

    peas (frozen)   basil, optional
    water or chicken stock*   butter
    sugar   flour
    salt

Using frozen peas is an acceptable compromise when fresh ones are not available. The following recipes have adapted traditional versions so that frozen peas may be substituted. (To use fresh peas in season, increase the liquid as necessary and add the peas with the other vegetables for a cooking time of 20 to 30 minutes, depending on the size and age of the peas.)

Cook the peas. Simmer gently for a few minutes only:
    2 cups (500 ml) frozen peas, defrosted,
    ¼ cup (60 ml) water or chicken stock (or add a piece of chicken
        jelly* to the cooking water),
    ¼ tsp. sugar,
    pinch salt,
    pinch basil, optional.

Thicken the cooking liquid. Mash together and stir into the peas:
    1–2 tsp. (5-10 g) butter,
    1 tsp. (5 g) flour.
Cook-stir a moment longer and serve.

Variation. Creamed Peas. Convert the basic recipe above by stirring into the thickened sauce
    1–2 Tbs. (15-30 ml) cream.
Cook to reduce slightly, then serve.

PEAS, COUNTRY STYLE ████████████████████████████████████

Ingredients

    peas (frozen)   chicken stock* or water
    salt pork   parsley
    butter   thyme
    pearl onions   pepper
    carrots   sugar
    flour

Blanch† the pork. Cut in a dice† and parboil† for 5 minutes
    2 oz. (60 g) salt pork.
Drain; rinse in cold water; dry.

Prepare the cooking liquid. Sauté the diced pork with:
>1 Tbs. (15 g) butter,
>10–12 pearl onions, peeled,
>2 large carrots, scraped and diced.

When lightly browned sprinkle with
>1 tsp. (5 g) flour.

Continue to cook a moment, then add:
>chicken stock or water to barely cover,
>3 sprigs parsley,
>pinch thyme,
>1–2 grinds pepper,
>½ tsp. sugar.

Cover the pan and simmer very gently for 15 to 20 minutes.

Add the peas. Stir in and simmer 10 minutes longer
>2 cups (500 ml) frozen, defrosted peas.

Remove the parsley; serve.

PEAS, FRENCH STYLE

Ingredients

peas	butter
chicken stock*	parsley
salt	pearl onions
sugar	Boston lettuce

French style peas are often served as a separate course in shallow soup plates.

Prepare the cooking liquid. Combine in a saucepan, cover and simmer for 15-20 minutes:
>¼ cup (60 ml) chicken stock,
>½ tsp. salt,
>1 Tbs. (15 g) sugar,
>1 Tbs. (15 g) butter,
>3 sprigs parsley,
>10 pearl onions, peeled,
>5–6 leaves Boston lettuce, shredded.

Add the peas. Stir into the cooking liquid and simmer 10 minutes longer.

CORN BRAISED IN CREAM

Ingredients

corn	light cream
salt and pepper	butter

Store-bought corn is always less than fresh but this cooking method makes up for much that is lost.

Preheat the oven 350 F (160 C).

Prepare the corn for cooking. Cut the kernels from

>   3 ears of corn.

Season with

>   salt and pepper, lightly sprinkled.

Toss lightly and spread the corn in a small, shallow baking dish. Pour over

>   ¼ cup (60 ml) light cream.

Cut into pieces and dot over the top

>   1 Tbs. (15 g) butter.

Bake the corn. Place in the preheated oven and bake for 30 minutes.

Braised Carrots, Glazed ▬▬▬▬▬▬▬▬▬▬▬▬▬▬▬

Ingredients

carrots	butter
brown beef or chicken stock*	sugar

Prepare the carrots for cooking. Place in a heavy saucepan:

>   2½ cups (625 ml) carrots, scraped and cut in serving-size pieces.

Add to the pan:

>   ⅔ to 1 cup (160-250 ml) beef or chicken stock (use the smaller amount for young, tender carrots),
>   1 Tbs. (15 g) butter,
>   ½ Tbs. (7 g) sugar.

Cook the carrots. Cover and simmer over very low heat until all the liquid has cooked away. Uncover and cook a little longer, shaking the pan to glaze the carrots with the syrupy residue in the bottom.

Variation. Creamed Carrots. Cook as above. When glazed pour in

>   ⅓ cup (80 ml) heavy cream.

Cook until the cream has reduced and thickened.

Braised Onions, Glazed ▬▬▬▬▬▬▬▬▬▬▬▬▬▬▬

Braised onions are cooked in the same manner as glazed carrots.

Prepare the onions for cooking. Peel small onions and pierce the base with an "x" (made with the point of a knife) to insure even cooking.

Add onions to the cooking liquid. Use a more diluted stock: half water and half stock. Herbs may also be cooked with the onions, if desired:

>   3 sprigs parsley,
>   ¼ domestic bay leaf,
>   pinch thyme.

Variation. Creamed Onions. Fold glazed onions into béchamel* or cream sauce.* Braised onions may also be served with Mornay,* curry sauce,* or sauce Espagnole.*

BRAISED TURNIPS

Ingredients

turnips	sugar
stock or water	salt
butter	parsley

Turnips go well with lamb, pork, or braised beef.

Prepare the turnips for cooking. In order to eliminate the slightly bitter flavor turnips sometimes have, parboil† in salted water for 5 minutes

 4–5 cups (1–1.25 l) white turnips,
 peeled, quartered.

Drain them and add

 ½–¾ cup (125-185 ml) stock or water.

Cook the turnips. Cover the pan and simmer for about 10 minutes. Remove the lid and cook until the liquid is reduced to about 2 Tbs. (30 ml). Roll the turnips around to glaze them and blend in:

 1 Tbs. (15 g) butter,
 1 tsp. (5 g) sugar.

Serve. Garnish turnips with chopped parsley.

Variation. Puréed Turnips. Put braised turnips through a ricer. Combine them with enough cream to give the consistency of puréed potatoes. They may also be combined with potatoes or carrots, cooked and puréed.

PASTA FAZOOL

Ingredients

pinto beans	garlic
meats, if desired, previously cooked	tomato
	parsley
oil	basil
butter	tomato paste
carrots	brown beef stock*
celery	salt
onion	large shell macaroni

This dish, containing grain and legume, could be a meal in itself. Bits of meat, especially ham, lamb, or veal, may also be added to simmer with the beans. If the meat has been previously cooked, add the meat only for reheating just before serving. Also include any pan sauce† or braising liquid that might be available to cook with the beans.

Prepare the beans for cooking. Wash well and soak overnight
    ½ lb. (225 g) pinto beans.

Or, see Cassoulet* for alternate preparation methods.

Prepare the seasonings. Cook together slowly in a heavy casserole:
    2 Tbs. (30 ml) oil,
    ½ Tbs. (8 g) butter,
    2 medium carrots, diced,
    2 small celery stalks (inner stalks and leaves), diced,
    ½ medium onion, diced.

When the onion is transparent, add and cook a few moments longer
    2 cloves garlic, crushed, peeled.

Blend in to season:
    1 medium tomato, peeled, seeded, chopped,
    2 sprigs parsley chopped,
    1 tsp. basil,
    1 Tbs. (15 ml) tomato paste.

Add:
    the beans and the water in which they were soaked,
    1½ cups (375 ml) beef stock,
    ½ tsp. salt.

Cook the beans. Bring the casserole to simmer. Cover, leaving a small space for steam to escape. Cook 1½ to 2 hours until the beans are tender.

Final steps. Mash the beans slightly and fold in
    1 cup (250 ml) large shell macaroni cooked al dente† in boiling, salted water; drained.

Serve. Garnish with chopped parsley.

SUGGESTIONS FOR OTHER BRAISED VEGETABLES

(1) *Braised Zucchini or Eggplant (Home Style).* This dish is treated in Italian Meatballs and Zucchini.*

(2) *Braised Sauerkraut.* Also called Choucroute Garni,* Braised Sauerkraut is described in the Ham section.

SAUTÉED VEGETABLES

SAUTÉED POTATOES ▬▬▬▬▬▬▬▬▬▬▬▬▬▬▬▬▬▬▬▬▬

Ingredients

    potatoes   parsley
    butter   salt
    oil

Prepare the potatoes for cooking. Select
> boiling type potatoes, counting 1–1½ large potatoes (before trimming) per serving.

Quarter each potato by cutting in half lengthwise and cutting each half of potato crosswise. With a small paring knife trim each quarter of potato into the shape of a large olive. Save all the cuttings for soup. (Cover them with water and cook them soon.)

Sauté the potatoes. Set a heavy skillet, large enough to contain the potatoes in one layer, over medium-high heat with:
> 2 Tbs. (30 g) butter,
> 2 Tbs. (30 ml) oil.

When the butter foams and begins to subside add the potatoes. Cook until seared, lightly browned on all sides.

Season the potatoes with
> salt, lightly sprinkled.

Cover the pan; reduce the heat. Cook about 15 minutes. Turn the potatoes 3 or 4 times so they will cook and brown evenly. Just before serving garnish with
> 1–2 sprigs parsley, minced.

SAUTÉED MUSHROOMS ▰▰▰▰▰▰▰▰▰▰▰▰▰▰▰

Ingredients

mushrooms	shallots or green onions
butter	salt and pepper
oil	

Browned mushrooms may accompany most dishes.

Prepare mushrooms for cooking. Wash, dry well and slice
> ½ lb (225 g) fresh mushrooms (with caps closed tightly to the stem).

Cook the mushrooms. Heat together in a heavy skillet over medium-high heat:
> 2 Tbs. (30 g) butter,
> 1 Tbs. (15 ml) oil.

After the butter foam begins to subside, stir in the mushrooms and sauté them quickly until lightly browned, stirring constantly for even cooking.

Add the seasonings. Stir in
> 2–3 shallots or green onions, minced.

Cook a moment longer. Season lightly with
> salt and pepper.

Variation. Fold sautéed mushrooms into béchamel sauce.*

MUSHROOM DUXELLES

Ingredients

mushrooms   Madeira
butter   thyme
shallot or green onion   allspice
salt and pepper

Duxelles provides a concentrated mushroom flavor when stirred into sauces, spread on canapés, used as a garnish, or blended into beaten eggs for omelets. It may be kept a week when refrigerated or it may be frozen for longer storage.

Cook the mushrooms. Melt in a small, heavy skillet
3 Tbs. (45 g) butter.
Add
½ lb. (225 g) mushrooms, washed, dried,
finely minced.
Cook uncovered on medium-low heat for half-an-hour, stirring occasionally. Reduce the heat to very low and cook for 1 hour. The mushrooms will have become darkened, dense, and quite reduced.

Season the duxelles. Stir in
1 shallot or green onion, minced.
Cook for 15 minutes. Season lightly with:
salt and pepper, lightly sprinkled,
1 Tbs. (15 ml) Madeira,
pinch each: thyme and allspice.
Cook 15 minutes longer for a total cooking time of 2 hours. Store in a jar and refrigerate or freeze.

SAUTÉED TOMATOES

Ingredients

tomatoes   oil
flour   salt
egg   fresh bread crumbs
milk

Prepare the tomatoes for cooking. Select
ripe, but firm tomatoes, about 1 to 1½ per serving.
Peel tomatoes. Cut in half; remove the seeds. Cut each half into 2 lengthwise slices. Give the slices an Anglaise coating:
(1) dip tomato slices in flour;
(2) coat slices in a mixture of:
1 egg,
4 Tbs. (60 ml) milk,

1 Tbs. (15 ml) oil,
½ tsp. salt;
(3) cover with fine, fresh bread crumbs.
Sauté the prepared tomatoes. Melt together in a heavy skillet over medium-high heat:
2 Tbs. (30 g) butter,
2 Tbs. (30 ml) oil.
When the butter foam nearly subsides, add the tomatoes and cook them quickly on both sides. Do not allow them to become soft from overcooking.
Note. For deep-fried zucchini or eggplant, peel the vegetable, then cut crosswise in ¾-inch (2 cm) slices. Coat Anglaise as described above. Fry in hot deep fat for a few seconds until the crumbs are golden brown. Accompany with a tomato sauce,* if desired.

BAKED VEGETABLES

BAKED TOMATOES STUFFED WITH DUXELLES ▬▬▬▬▬▬▬▬▬

Ingredients

tomatoes	dry bread crumbs and Swiss
mushroom duxelles*	cheese topping
fresh bread crumbs or	butter

Preheat the oven 400 F (185 C).
Prepare tomatoes for baking. Select
ripe, but firm tomatoes, 1 per serving.
Peel tomatoes; cut in half crosswise. Remove the seeds with forefinger. To eliminate excess juice in tomatoes hold each half in the palm of the hand. Close hand and gently squeeze. The tomato must not be crushed and should be carefully returned to its original shape. Fill the spaces left by the seeds with
mushroom duxelles.
Cover the tops of the tomatoes with either
fresh bread crumbs or a mixture of dry bread crumbs and Swiss
cheese.
Drizzle over the topping
melted butter.
Bake the tomatoes. Set in the preheated oven and cook for 20 minutes.
Variation. Tomatoes Provençal. Follow the directions above for preparing and baking the tomatoes. For an alternate filling prepare for every 2 large tomatoes:
1 Tbs. (15 g) butter simmered with
1 clove garlic, minced.

Stir in:
>   1 sprig parsley, minced,
>   pinch basil,
>   1 slice bread, reduced to crumbs.

POTATOES DAUPHINOISE (FRENCH BAKED POTATOES) ▰▰▰▰▰▰

Ingredients

potatoes	butter
salt and pepper	milk
Swiss cheese	

This recipe and its variation use the traditional French method for baking potatoes. Potatoes are first peeled, then combined with a liquid which is absorbed during baking. Strictly speaking, it is not necessary to peel the potatoes. For everyday cooking that step may be eliminated if the potatoes are first scrubbed very well with a brush.

Preheat the oven 400 F (185 C).

Prepare the potatoes for cooking. Peel and slice thinly
>   4 medium baking (Idaho-type) potatoes.

Layer half of the potatoes in a buttered, shallow baking dish. Season with:
>   salt and pepper, lightly sprinkled,
>   ½ cup (125 ml) grated Swiss cheese (grate 1 cup (250 ml) cheese in all),
>   1 Tbs. (15 g) butter, cut into dots (need 2 Tbs. (30 g) in all).

Lay over the remaining potatoes; season with salt, pepper, remaining cheese and butter. Pour over
>   1 cup (250 ml) hot milk.

Bake the casserole. Set in preheated oven and bake for 30–40 minutes.

Variation. Garlic or Onion Baked Potatoes. Gently simmer the 2 Tbs. (30 g) butter with a large clove of garlic (crushed, peeled, minced) or 2 large green onions (minced) for 2 to 3 minutes without permitting it to brown. Proceed with the above recipe.

POTATOES BAKED WITH TOMATO SAUCE AND BACON ▰▰▰▰▰▰

Ingredients

bacon	parsley
butter	potatoes
onion	brown beef stock*
tomatoes	salt and pepper

Preheat the oven 400 F (185 C).

Prepare the sauce. In a small skillet render until lightly browned

3 slices bacon cut into 8 crosscut pieces.

Drain the bacon on paper towels. Pour out the bacon fat and add to the skillet:

2 Tbs. (30 g) butter,

1 small onion, sliced.

Sauté until the onion is lightly browned. Add

2 medium tomatoes, peeled, seeded, chopped.

Cook until the tomatoes are somewhat reduced. Add

2 sprigs parsley, chopped.

Assemble the casserole. Peel and slice in ¼-inch (.5 cm) slices

3–4 baking potatoes.

Layer tomato sauce, potatoes, and bacon in a buttered shallow baking dish, ending with potatoes. Season each layer very lightly with

salt and pepper.

Pour over

½ cup (125 ml) beef stock.

Bake in preheated oven for 30 to 40 minutes.

Variation. Mediterranean Baked Potatoes. Omit the bacon; fold into the tomato sauce:

2–4 anchovies, mashed,

pinch each: basil, thyme,

1 clove garlic, crushed, peeled.

Arrange in a baking dish as described above. Sprinkle over the top:

¼ cup (60 ml) grated Swiss cheese, then

1 tsp. oil.

Note. Convert the chilled remains of the recipes above to a potato salad by combining with a vinaigrette sauce.* French potato salad is treated in Veal Salad Parisian Style.*

Steambaked Potatoes ▐███████████████████████████▌

This sequence of potato recipes is based on a new method. Most of potatoes' vitamins are found just beneath the skin and are lost to the water if potatoes are peeled and boiled. The new process for puréed potatoes and related recipes begins with baking potatoes in a manner that renders the skins pliable and easy to remove and is called steambaking.

Ingredients

potatoes
salt
butter

Preheat the oven 350 F (160 C).

Preparation steps. Lightly butter a baking dish that has a matching lid and is deep enough to contain the potatoes. For each serving wash
a medium, Idaho-type potato.

Do not dry the skins but place them, wet, in the baking dish. Season each potato lightly with:
salt,
a dot of butter.

Steambake the potatoes. Place the lid on the casserole and set in the preheated oven. Bake for 1 hour.

Serve. Potatoes may be served as they are, or peeled and sliced, or puréed as described below.

CREAMED POTATOES ▐███▌

Ingredients

steambaked potatoes (above)	salt and pepper
cream	butter

Steambake potatoes. Following the directions above prepare
1 Idaho-type potato per serving.

Peel the potatoes. Hold the hot potatoes firmly in a tongs held in one hand. With the aid of a small pointed knife pull away the skin. Slice the potatoes into a heavy saucepan and add:
cream to almost cover,
salt and pepper to taste.

Cook uncovered until the cream is reduced to about half. Just before serving spread over
1 Tbs. (15 g) butter.

Variation. Creamed Potatoes with Sausage. Layer in a buttered casserole in the order given:
sliced, peeled, steambaked potatoes,
slices of onion, sautéed in butter,
slices or small patties of sausage,
more sautéed onion,
another layer of potatoes.

Prepare and pour over:
béchamel sauce* seasoned with
salt and pepper,
pinch each of marjoram, parsley, nutmeg.

Shake the sauce through to the bottom. Spread over the top:
grated Swiss cheese,
dots of butter.

Bake 1 hour, 350 F (160 C).

PURÉED STEAMBAKED POTATOES

Ingedients

steambaked potatoes*   butter
milk   salt

The value of steambaked potatoes is readily evident in this purée recipe. They are not watery and are surprisingly full of flavor.

Steambake potatoes. Prepare as described above
   1 baking potato per serving.
Prepare the liquid. Scald together in a deep-sided stainless steel pan ¼ cup (60 ml) milk for *each* potato.
For *every four* potatoes add to the pan:
   1 Tbs. (15 g) butter,
   1 tsp. (5 g) salt.
Rice the potatoes. Cut each potato in half. One at a time, place potato halves in a ricer, cut side down. Force the pulp through the ricer letting the potato fall into the hot milk mixture in the saucepan. Remove the skin from the basket of the ricer. Repeat until all the potatoes have been riced.
Serve. Whip the potatoes by hand or with an electric hand mixer.

DUCHESS POTATOES

Ingredients

steambaked potatoes*   salt and pepper
eggs   nutmeg

This is a stiffer version of puréed potatoes used for piping decorative borders.

Steambake potatoes. Prepare as directed above
   1 baking potato per serving.
Rice the potatoes. Following the directions given for puréed potatoes, pass them through a ricer, letting the riced pulp fall into a bowl. For *every four* medium-sized potatoes whip in:
   1 whole egg,
   1 egg yolk,
   1 tsp. (5 g) salt,
   2–3 grinds pepper,
   dash nutmeg.
Variation. Potato Cakes. Remaining duchess potatoes may be used this way or prepare them as described above omitting, if desired, the extra egg

yolk. Shape into patties and chill. Just before cooking, coat each patty by dipping it successively into:

    (1) flour,

    (2) beaten egg,

    (3) dry bread crumbs.

Heat in a heavy skillet on medium to medium-high heat

    2 Tbs. (30 g) *each* of butter and oil.

When the butter foams and begins to subside, add the cakes. Sauté† them quickly until lightly browned on both sides.

BAKED BEETS

Ingredients

    beets

    butter

    salt and pepper

Beets may be served with beef, pork, and poultry.

Preheat the oven 350 F (160 C).

Prepare for cooking. Select

    1–2 beets per serving, depending on size.

Wash the beets taking care not to break their skins. Cut off the green tops leaving ½-inch (1 cm) stems on the beet root.

Steambake the beets. Follow the directions for Steambaked Potatoes.* Cook for 45 to 60 minutes in the preheated oven. Beets are done when they are tender when pierced with a fork.

Peel the beets. Drop beets into a large bowl filled with cold water. Simply rub them to remove skins and stems. Dice the beets or cut into slices.

Serve. Combine with:

    melted butter,

    salt and pepper, lightly to taste.

Variations. (1) Creamed Beets. Fold diced or sliced steambaked beets into a béchamel sauce.*

(2) Beets, Flemish Style. Cook together in a saucepan:

    1 Tbs. (15 g) butter,

    ½ small onion, minced.

Sprinkle over and cook to a very light brown

    1 Tbs. (15 g) flour.

Pour in

    ¾ cup (185 ml) hot chicken stock.

Season the sauce with:

    2 Tbs. (30 ml) mild red wine vinegar,

    2 tsp. (10 g) sugar,

    ½ tsp. salt,

    2–3 grinds pepper.

Fold in
  steambaked beets, sliced or diced.
Let stand a few minutes before reheating to serve.

STUFFED VEGETABLES

When a vegetable is stuffed and baked, both the vegetable and the filling benefit from the exchange of flavors. The charts on the following pages describe the preparation required of the vegetable and suggest possible combinations for filling mixtures.

Grains

POLENTA ██

Ingredients

water   butter
salt   Swiss or Parmesan cheese
yellow corn meal

Corn meal provides an interesting change from potatoes and rice. Italian polenta has several flexible variations for serving as a main dish.

Cook the corn meal. Bring to boiling:
  4 cups (1 l) water,
  ½ tsp. salt.
Stir in
  1 cup (250 ml) yellow corn meal.
Continue stirring with a wire whip over medium heat until no lumps remain. Reduce the heat to very low and cook for 30 minutes. Stir the polenta well with a wooden spoon about every 5 minutes. Remove from the heat and blend in:
  2 Tbs. (30 g) butter,
  ¼ cup (60 ml) grated Swiss or Parmesan cheese.

SERVING SUGGESTIONS

(1) *Italian home style polenta.* Simply transfer polenta to a serving dish after adding butter and cheese.

(2) *Polenta with sausages.* Spread the polenta into an even layer in a shallow pan and let it cool and set. Then, cut into squares or diamond shapes. Arrange the pieces of polenta on individual heat-proof dishes; brush with melted butter. Reheat in a hot oven at 450 F (210 C) for 10 or 15 minutes with small, previously browned sausages.

(3) *Cheese polenta.* Squares of polenta may be layered in a buttered baking dish with butter and grated Swiss cheese over each layer. Reheat 30 minutes before serving time in a 350 F (160 C) oven. Serve with roast pork, chops, or chicken.

Stuffed Vegetable Preparation

(1) *Artichokes.* Stem, trim, and parboil† 10 minutes. Drain; remove the choke. Stuff and braise in stock to ⅓ cover. Oven: 350 F (160 C); 45-60 minutes.

(2) *Cabbage Leaves.* Remove the large outer leaves by severing each leaf at its base and easing it away from the head. Drop one at a time in boiling water for a few seconds until the leaf is pliable. Put a spoonful of filling on the leaf; roll envelope style. Place rolls in casserole on a bed of sliced carrot and sautéed onion. Braise in stock to ⅓ cover. Remaining cabbage may be chopped and added to stock. Oven: 350 F (160 C); 1-1½ hours.

(3) *Eggplant.* Split in half lengthwise. Cut 3 or 4 lengthwise gashes to within ¼ inch (.5 cm) of the skin. Salt cut surfaces to draw out moisture for 30 minutes. Scoop out pulp with a sharp spoon. Stuff, using some of the pulp squeezed of excess moisture. Brush outside with oil. Bake uncovered: 350 F (160 C); 30-45 minutes.

(4) *Lettuce.* One stuffed lettuce serves 1 or 2. Carefully remove the central, tightly clustered leaves from Boston lettuce, leaving the base and outer leaves intact. (Use inner leaves for salad.) Blanch† outer leaves and attached base 1 to 2 minutes in boiling water until wilted. Carefully drain. Place filling on base in a mound. Draw leaves up over filling. Lay strips of blanched bacon over stuffed lettuces. Arrange them in a casserole on a bed of sliced, sautéed† onion and carrot. Add stock and tomatoes, peeled and seeded, to come 2 inches (5 cm) up inside the lettuce. Cover; braise in oven 350 F (160 C); 45–60 minutes.

(5) *Onions.* Peel and remove centers of large onions with a sharp knife. Parboil† 10 minutes. Sauté some of the center, chopped, in butter and include with the stuffing. Fill onions. Add stock to ⅓ cover. Bake uncovered 350 F (160 C); 30 minutes. Baste often.

(6) *Peppers.* Parboil† whole peppers 3–5 minutes. Cut off tops; discard inner pulp and seeds. Stuff and brush skins with oil. Bake in open pan at 350 F (160 C); 35-45 minutes.

(7) *Potatoes.* Scrub; split lengthwise and scoop out centers. Include some of the potato, diced, in the filling. Rub skins with soft butter. Bake in open pan at 350 F (160 C); 35-45 minutes.

(8) *Squash.* Split winter acorn squash lengthwise (stem to blossom end). Scrape out and discard seeds. Stuff and bake in oven: 350 F (160 C); 45-50 minutes.

(9) *Turnips.* Peel and parboil† for 8 minutes. Scoop out centers with a sharp spoon; stuff using some of the pulp. Bake uncovered in stock to ⅓ cover. Oven: 350 F (160 C). Baste often.

(10) *Zucchini.* Scrub and split in half lengthwise. Sprinkle cut surfaces with salt and let set for 30 minutes to draw out moisture. Scoop out centers with a sharp spoon. Stuff, incorporating some of the pulp squeezed of excess moisture. Brush outside with oil. Bake uncovered. Oven: 350 F (160 C); 30 minutes.

Filling Mixture Combinations

(1) *Meat.* Chopped or ground, uncooked; or combine previously cooked meat with an equal part of uncooked meat (for instance, 1 part ground, roasted beef and 1 part pork sausage). Use veal, beef, pork, ham, sausage, lamb, or chicken.

(2) *Additional vegetables.* Use pulp of the container vegetable and if desired nuts (almonds, pinenuts) and mushroom duxelles.*

(3) *Seasonings.* Finely chopped onion, garlic, carrot, or celery cooked in butter; salt and pepper; parsley and other herbs.

(4) *Binder.* Egg or crustless bread soaked in milk or stock and squeezed dry.

(5) *Extender.* If necessary add cooked noodles, rice, or bread croutons, sautéed in butter.

~ ~ ~ ~ ~ ~ ~ ~ ~ ~ ~

Toppings

(1) *Cheese,* cut in slices *or*

(2) *Cheese,* grated and combined with dry bread crumbs with dots of butter *or*

(3) *Butter,* melted.

~ ~ ~ ~ ~ ~ ~ ~ ~ ~ ~

Sauces for Stuffed Vegetables

Use tomato sauce,* sauce Espagnole,* béchamel,* or any suitable variation of these sauces.

(4) *Main dish.* As an aid in using previously cooked meats, polenta is sometimes arranged in a buttered baking dish in alternate layers with creamed meat mixtures: braised† or roasted† beef, veal, or chicken ground and combined with béchamel* or Mornay sauce.* Begin and end with a layer of polenta. Sprinkle grated Swiss cheese over the top and dot with butter. Reheat in 375 F (170 C) oven for 30 minutes.

Note. Gnocchi, similar to polenta, is treated in Chicken Gnocchi, Gamba.*

RICE (RISOTTO)

Ingredients

> long grain white rice
> butter
> salt

The method outlined below is the most effective for producing non-sticky rice that is easily adaptable to variations.

Initial steps. Melt in a heavy saucepan
>   2 Tbs. (30 g) butter.

Add
>   1 cup (250 ml) long grain white rice.

Cook and stir over medium to medium-high heat until the rice turns a chalky white but is not browned.

Add the liquid. Remove the pan from the heat. Pour in:
>   2 cups (500 ml) hot water,
>   ¼ tsp. salt.

Return the pan to the heat and bring quickly to boiling. Stir through to the bottom of the pan.

Simmer the rice. Cover the pan and reduce the heat to the lowest setting. Simmer the rice for 15 minutes. Turn off the heat and leave the pan undisturbed to steam for 15 minutes longer.

Serve. Quickly invert the pan over the serving bowl and let the rice drop all at once into the dish. Do not scrape the pan to remove the grains that adhere to the bottom. Toss the rice with two forks to dry and separate the grains. Serve at once.

Variations. (1) Pilaff. Cook 1 Tbs. (15 ml) minced onion in the butter before adding the rice. Substitute stock for water. Garnish, to serve, with chopped parsley.

(2) Piedmont Style. Cook ½ small onion, minced, in the butter before adding the rice. Substitute stock blended with 1 Tbs. (15 ml) tomato paste for the water. When cooked, toss the rice with grated Swiss cheese to serve.

Rounding Out the Meal

This chapter brings us full circle. The following sections on hors d'oeuvre, soup, and eggs adapt and expand methods and recipes already developed in previous chapters. Dessert dishes are also built on skills outlined in preceding chapters, especially on formulas for crêpes, pastry, and soufflés. The recipes in this collection are, above all, flexible; thus the pastry dough and crêpe batter may work as well for desserts or hors d'oeuvre as for main dishes. Sweet soufflés are developed from a procedure that simply modifies the basic technique in Chapter 5.

A concern for good cooking and wholesome eating has a very positive effect on an overall diet pattern. Most overweight problems are caused by eating between meals and high-carbohydrate desserts. In this book, we emphasize preparing excellent main dishes with one or two accompanying courses. A fully satisfying meal obviates the need for rich desserts and cravings for between-meal snacks disappear. Serving salad *after* the main course to "lighten" the meal also tends to curb the desire for something sweet.

From the standpoint of nutrition and diet, Americans might try the French preference for a dessert of fruit and cheese as a light, after-dinner treat. A list of cheese suggestions is included in the closing section. The entries to follow were chosen for practicality, adaptability, and lightness, with only a passing interest given to "sweetness."

Hors d'Oeuvre

It is quite possible to make a meal of hors d'oeuvre alone. In hot weather especially, a pâté, a quiche, vegetables in vinaigrette, and melon would be a lovely, satisfying meal, and easy to take on a picnic. However as a general rule, hors d'oeuvre should be small, piquant servings calculated to whet rather than satiate the appetite.

Most hors d'oeuvre can be made well in advance of dinner: a pastry, days ahead; sauces, early in the day; croquettes mixtures may chill for

153

hours; prepared canapés can await reheating for one or two hours. A clever cook will use the hors d'oeuvre tray to "finish up" small amounts of foods not utilized in other ways. Some of the suggestions below adapt ideas from other chapters in this book.

Serving Suggestions: Hors d'Oeuvre Tray

Chilled Selections. (1) *Fruit.* Select melons in season or fresh pineapple.

(2) *Vegetables, au naturel.* Use uncooked vegetables cut in attractive serving pieces.

(3) *Cooked vegetables.* Chill and serve with Dijon mustard sauce.*

(4) *Meat or fish.* Cook, chill, slice and serve appropriately sauced.

(5) *Cabbage rolls.* Serve cold with vinaigrette sauce.*

(6) *Composed salads.* Make scaled-down versions of the rice or potato salads (consult the Index).

(7) *Spreads.* Make of ground or minced meat; season and serve on canapés or with crackers.

(8) *Stuffed eggs.* Use deviled eggs or fill with canned pâté, or chicken liver pâté (below), or caviar.

(9) *Canned specialties combinations:* (a) *sardines,* hard-boiled eggs, English mustard, wheat toasts; (b) *smoked salmon,* lemon juice, pepper, capers, sweet buttered black bread; (c) *anchovy filet,* pimento green olive slices, sautéed canapés; (d) *caviar* topping a wedge of cream cheese and slice of cucumber on pumpernickle crackers.

Hot hors d'oeuvre. (1) *Cheese fritters.**

(2) *Mushroom duxelles.** Spread on crackers.

(3) *Creamed spreads.* Combine any chopped meats, cheese, fish, or shellfish with béchamel sauce* to hold it together and spread on canapés.

(4) *Tartlettes.* Fill with sauced meat, fish, shellfish, or chicken.

(5) *Miniature "pastys."* Make tiny pastry turnovers; fill with small pieces of cheese or seasoned, ground meat. Bake or deep-fry.

(6) *Tiny-sized croquettes.** Make with fish, shellfish, veal, chicken or liver. Cut creamed mixture into small cubes, shape into balls, coat and deep-fry.

(7) *Crêpes.* Make half-size, or cut in half, and fill with a savory mixture.

Chicken Liver Pâté

Ingredients

butter	ground cloves
shallots or green onions	salt and pepper
chicken livers	thyme
Cognac	ginger
Madeira	cinnamon
eggs	marjoram

Cook the livers. Cook together very slowly in a small skillet until the shallot is transparent:

> 4 Tbs. (60 g) butter,
> 2 shallots or 3 green onions, minced.

Add and continue to cook gently without browning:

> ½ lb. (225 g) chicken livers, filaments removed, and chopped,
> ½ domestic bay leaf.

After a few moments, before the livers have stiffened, add and simmer to evaporate the alcohol:

> 1 Tbs. (15 ml) Cognac,
> 1 Tbs. (15 ml) Madeira.

When the chicken livers are just firm but still very tender, remove the pan from the heat and take out the bay leaf.

Season the livers. In a bowl beat until creamy

> 4 Tbs. (60 g) butter.

Add to the creamed butter, blending well:

> the cooked livers and their cooking juices,
> 2 small (or 1½ large) eggs, hard-boiled, chopped,
> pinch ground cloves,
> 2–3 grinds pepper,
> ⅛ tsp. each: salt, thyme, ginger,
> cinnamon, marjoram.

Final steps. Scrape the mixture into a blender jar and purée. Pack the pâté into a sterile half-pint (250 ml) jar. Cover and chill thoroughly before serving.

QUICHE LORRAINE ▐▬▬▬▬▬▬▬▬▬▬▬▬▬▬▬▬▬▬▬

Ingredients

pastry*	salt
bacon	nutmeg
Swiss cheese	milk
eggs	cream
flour	butter

Prepare the pastry. Make in advance and have chilling in the refrigerator

> pastry.

Before preparing the filling, roll the pastry out and fit into an 8-inch (20 cm) pie pan or flan ring. Return to the refrigerator.

Preheat the oven 375 F (170 C).

Prepare the filling. Render and sauté in its own fat until browned, but not too done

> 6 slices bacon, chopped.

Lift the bacon from the skillet with a slotted spoon and drain on paper towels. Prepare

> ⅔ cup (160 ml) Swiss cheese cut in ½-inch (1 cm) dice.

In a bowl beat together in the order given, blending well:

 3 eggs, beaten,
 1 Tbs. (15 g) flour,
 ½ tsp. salt,
 pinch nutmeg,
 1½ cups (375 ml) milk,
 ½ cup (125 ml) cream,
 ½ Tbs. (8 g) butter, melted and very lightly browned.

Complete the quiche. Remove the pastry shell from the refrigerator and prick the sides and bottom with the tines of a fork at ½-inch (1 cm) intervals. Spread the bacon in the bottom of the shell. Arrange the cheese over the bacon. Pour over the egg-milk mixture. Bake in the preheated oven for 30 to 35 minutes or until the custard is set and the top is puffed and nicely browned.

Variation. Shellfish Quiche. This alternate is a much lighter filling than the preceding one and is a good first course for roast beef or lamb dinner. Cook together, slowly, in a small, heavy skillet:

 1 Tbs. (15 g) butter,
 1 shallot or white of 1 large green onion.

When the onion is transparent add:

 1 sprig parsley, minced,
 ½ tsp. tarragon,
 1 cup (250 ml) cooked shellfish.

Stir to blend the flavors. Add:

 ¼ cup (60 ml) dry white wine.

Simmer just a moment; remove from the heat. Beat together in a bowl:

 3 eggs,
 1 Tbs. (15 ml) flour,
 1 tsp. Dijon mustard,
 1 cup (250 ml) milk,
 ½ cup (125 ml) cream,
 ½ tsp. salt,
 1–2 grinds pepper.

Scrape the contents of the skillet into the egg-milk mixture in the bowl and blend. Pour into a pastry shell and bake as described above.

Note. Ham and Potato Pie* baked in a pastry could also be served as a quiche.

Soups

Generally, we do not fully utilize the many ways to serve and enjoy soups. While everyone thinks of a hearty soup as a comforting meal, we forget that a small cup of soup is a gratifying addition to almost any meal. Soup takes little time or effort to make and is the perfect solution for using up small amounts of vegetables and meats. Even spoonfuls of leftover sauces may be used to flavor and enrich soups.

This section shows how to adapt pan sauces from braised and roasted meats to make stock-based soups. There is also a flexible formula which can be adjusted to make crème soups from practically any vegetable. This, after all, is the whole idea of soup; the dish is open to many variations to accommodate tastes, menus, and available foods.

VEGETABLE SOUPS

LEEK OR ONION AND POTATO SOUP

Ingredients

butter	salt and pepper
leeks or onions	cream
potatoes	parsley or chives

Leeks always give a much finer flavor to this soup than onions, but they are only seasonally available in most markets.

Prepare the soup. Cook together slowly until tender but not browned:
   1 Tbs. (15 g) butter,
   whites of 3 leeks, thinly sliced, *or*
   1 large yellow onion, diced.
Add:
   6 cups (1.5 l) water,
   4 medium potatoes, cut in ½-inch (1 cm) dice,
   1 tsp. (5 g) salt.
Cover partially and simmer for 30 to 40 minutes until the potatoes are soft. Mash the potatoes slightly with a fork to thicken the soup. Enrich with
   ⅓ cup (80 ml) cream.
Correct the seasoning with:
   salt, to taste,
   few grinds of pepper.
Serve. Garnish with:
   chopped parsley or chives.
Variations. (1) Vichyssoise. To convert this soup to the famous cold soup version, strain it through a sieve before adding the cream. Press the potatoes through the sieve; add the cream and an equal amount of milk. Reheat the soup, stirring; then strain it again and chill. Garnish and serve.

(2) Potato Soup in Stock. Cook the vegetables in brown beef stock* instead of water. Omit the cream and enrich with 1 Tbs. (15 g) butter.

VEGETABLE SOUP OF LORRAINE ▬▬▬▬▬▬▬▬▬▬▬

Ingredients

dried white beans	cabbage
onion	celery
leeks, if available	thyme
garlic	bay leaf
butter	salt and pepper
carrots	rounds of dried French bread
potatoes	cream
turnips	parsley

This is a good weekend soup: lunch for a busy Saturday or a light, but satisfying, Sunday evening supper.

Prepare the soup. Soak overnight
    ¼ cup (60 ml) dried white beans.
Cook together slowly without browning:
    1 small onion, diced,
    whites of 2 leeks, sliced, if available,
    1 clove garlic,
    ? Tbs. (45 g) butter.
Add the vegetables and butter, and the soaked beans to
    2½ qts. (2.5 l) boiling water in a soup kettle.
Also add these vegetables, peeled, but left whole:
    4 medium carrots,
    3 medium potatoes,
    3 turnips.
Wash, trim and add:
    1 very small head of cabbage (left whole) with an "X" pierced in its
        base to encourage even cooking,
    2–4 stalks celery.
Season with:
    pinch thyme,
    ¼ domestic bay leaf,
    salt and pepper to taste.
Partially cover the kettle and simmer the vegetables for 1 hour until the vegetables are just tender and full of flavor.

Serve. Heat a soup tureen and cover the bottom with:
    slices of French bread, dried and lightly toasted.
Pour over the bread:
    ½ cup (125 ml) cream,
    3 sprigs parsley, chopped.
Strain the soup broth over the bread in the tureen. Arrange the vegetables in a large serving dish to accompany the soup. Place the cabbage in the center of the dish; split it open in quarter sections and insert
    a piece of butter

to melt in the cabbage. Cut the other vegetables in halves or quarters and place them around the cabbage. At the table, ladle the broth and bread into soup plates and pass the vegetables separately.

CLEAR STOCK-BASED SOUPS

FRENCH ONION SOUP

Ingredients

onions	salt and pepper
butter	Cognac
oil	dry white wine
flour	rounds of dried French bread
brown beef stock*	Swiss cheese
tomato paste	

Cook the onions. Cook together slowly in a covered pan for 10 minutes:

> 3 medium yellow onions, sliced,
> 2 Tbs. (30 g) butter,
> 1 Tbs. (15 ml) oil.

Remove the cover and continue cooking the onions over medium to medium-low heat, stirring frequently, until they are richly browned. This will require about 30 minutes of cooking.

Finish the soup. Sprinkle over the onions and cook until browned

> 1 Tbs. (15 g) flour.

Pour over, whisking to blend

> 2 qts. (2 l) boiling stock: a rich, brown homemade stock* or stock from a pot-au-feu.

Bring the soup to simmering and season with:

> 1 tsp. tomato paste,
> salt and pepper, to taste,
> 1 Tbs. (15 ml) Cognac,
> ½ cup (125 ml) dry white wine.

Simmer the soup for 30 to 40 minutes.

Garnish. Place in a heated soup tureen:

> toasted slices of French bread,
> ½ cup (125 ml) grated Swiss cheese.

Pour the hot onion soup over the bread and cheese, and serve.

BEEF CONSOMMÉ

Ingredients

brown beef stock*	chopped beef
green onion	egg whites
parsley	

Prepare the stock. The stock for consommé must first have been chilled and had every trace of fat removed from its surface. Heat on low to liquify
>   4 cups (1 l) homemade beef stock.

Clarify the stock. Beat together:
>   2 egg whites,
>   1–2 oz. (30-60 g) beef, trimmed of all fat, chopped,
>   leaf tops of 1 green onion, chopped,
>   2–3 sprigs parsley, minced.

Stir into the stock and bring it slowly, stirring, just to the boil. Then simmer, not stirring, until the white is coagulated. Skim out the masses of white with a slotted spoon and strain the stock through several thicknesses of cheesecloth.

Variation. Tomato Consommé. Add to the clarified consommé prepared as above
>   1 large ripe tomato, peeled, seeded, chopped.

Simmer together 10 minutes. Serve hot or cold. Garnish with
>   paper-thin slices of lemon.

OUTLINE FOR PAN SAUCE SOUPS

A simple savory soup may be created from the concentrated flavor of pan sauces from any roasted or braised meat or poultry. Even less than a cup of sauce is a sufficient amount for soup base.

Prepare the base. Dilute with water in these proportions:
>   1 part pan sauce, all fat removed from its surface,
>   3 parts water.

Add an assortment of any of these vegetables, peeled if necessary, and uniformly sliced or diced:
>   asparagus, carrots, onions, potatoes, leeks, mushrooms, tomatoes, parsnips, cauliflower, green beans, celery, turnips, zucchini or other squash.

For added body you may include
>   several pieces of broken pasta, rice, or barley.

Season with:
>   salt and pepper to taste,
>   small pinch thyme or other herbs.

Simmer together about 40 minutes.

Final steps. Any of these vegetables may be added the last 10 or 15 minutes of cooking:
>   cabbage, Brussels sprouts, broccoli, spinach, watercress, frozen and defrosted peas or limas,
>   any previously cooked vegetables and their cooking liquid.

At the last minute taste for seasoning and stir in
    chopped parsley,
and enrich with
    ½ Tbs. (8 g) butter, optional.

OUTLINE FOR CRÈME SOUPS

This formula uses wheat flour instead of the traditional rice flour to thicken the soup base. The first step is to make a thick Velouté sauce* to give body to the soup; this may be done well in advance.

Prepare the chicken stock base. Cook together over low heat until the onion is transparent:
    3 Tbs. (45 g) butter,
    ½ small onion, minced.
Make a roux† by blending in and cooking 1 to 2 minutes
    3 Tbs. (45 g) flour.
Pour in, whisking to blend
    1 cup (250 ml) hot chicken stock* or pan sauce† from previously
      cooked chicken mixed with water.
Cook-stir 2 or 3 minutes longer.

Separately prepare the flavor ingredient. Simmer together 15–30 minutes until the vegetables are tender:
    1 cup (250 ml) of a vegetable: asparagus, peas, celery, carrots,
      cauliflower, spinach or watercress and/or
    mushrooms cooked separately in a little water and lemon juice,
    1½ cups (375 ml) water or chicken stock,*
    2 leaves Boston lettuce, shredded.
Add an herb bouquet:
    1 stalk celery,
    2 sprigs parsley,
    pinch thyme,
    ¼ domestic bay leaf.

Purée the vegetables. When the vegetables are tender, remove the herbs and process with the stock in a blender. Or, force the vegetables through a sieve or a food mill.

Final steps. At the last minute combine the cooked vegetables with the soup base. Heat the soup to steaming, whisking to smooth. Season and enrich the soup with:
    2 Tbs. (30 ml) cream,
    salt and pepper, lightly to taste.

Serve. Garnish with
    chopped herbs or parsley or a few vegetables saved from the stock
      before puréeing.

CRÈME OF TOMATO SOUP

Ingredients

crème soup base (above)	cream
tomatoes	cooked rice or spaghetti
chicken stock*	salt and pepper
tomato paste	

Make the crème soup base. Follow the directions given above for chicken stock base.

Prepare the tomatoes. Cook together until reduced to 2 cups (500 ml):
    3 large tomatoes, chopped,
    ¼ cup (60 ml) chicken stock.
Force the cooked tomatoes through a potato ricer to separate the pulp. Discard the tomato skins. For color, add to the tomato pulp
    1 Tbs. (15 ml) tomato paste.

Final steps. Just before serving combine the tomato pulp with the soup base and simmer a few minutes, whisking to smooth. Enrich and season the soup with:
    2 Tbs. (30 ml) cream,
    salt and pepper to taste.

Serve. Garnish with
    few grains cooked rice, or
    broken spaghetti, cooked.

SHRIMP BISQUE

Ingredients

crème soup base*	thyme
butter	bay leaf
carrot	dry white wine
onion	Cognac
parsley	shrimp

Make the crème soup base. Follow the directions given above for chicken stock base, using only ¼ of a small onion to season it.

Prepare the shrimp. Cook together slowly in a covered pan until tender:
    1 Tbs. (15 g) butter,
    1 Tbs. (15 ml) carrot, finely diced,
    1 Tbs. (15 ml) onion, finely diced,
    1 sprig parsley,
    small pinch thyme,
    ¼ domestic bay leaf.

When the vegetables are tender add:
> ½ cup (125 ml) dry white wine,
> 12 well-washed shrimp.

Gently poach the shrimp for 8 minutes. Remove them from the liquid and shell and devein. Save the shells and reserve 6 shrimp for the garnish.

Finish the stock. Finely chop the shells and remaining shrimp; return them to the poaching liquid. Add
> 1½ cups (375 ml) chicken stock.

Simmer for 20 minutes. Strain the stock through a fine sieve.

Final steps. At the last minute combine the strained stock with the soup base. Reheat to steaming, whisking to smooth. Thin with
> 1–2 Tbs. (15-30 ml) milk.

Strain again. Taste for
> salt and pepper.

Bring the bisque nearly to boiling. Stir in:
> 1 Tbs. (15 g) butter,
> 1 Tbs. (15 ml) Cognac.

Serve immediately with the garnish of diced shrimp.

Note. Other heartier meat and vegetable soups may be found in the meat chapter; see:
Petite Marmite,* Mediterranean Soup,* Split Pea Soup.*

Eggs for the First Course

Any of the following dishes could serve as a main course by allowing two eggs per serving and elaborating with substantial garnitures (*e.g.*, sausages, chicken livers, or tomatoes which have been peeled, stuffed with creamed mixtures, and baked). These dishes also make excellent light luncheons or suppers. However, as entrées to a meal, allow just one egg for each portion.

METHOD FOR HARD-BOILED EGGS

Cook the eggs. Place eggs in a saucepan and cover with cold water to twice the depth of the eggs. Set the pan on medium-high to high heat. Stir the eggs now and then to keep the yolks centered. Bring the water just to a gentle boil; then, turn off the heat and cover the pan. In 20 minutes pour off the water and run cold water over the eggs.

Peel the eggs. Gently tap each end of the egg to crack the shell and return it to the cold water. After about 10 minutes' rest the cooked egg will have shrunk from its shell. Crack the entire surface of the shell and peel it away. Rinse the egg to remove any traces of shell or membrane. The eggs are now ready to be sauced.

EGGS CHIMAY

Ingredients

hard-boiled eggs (above)	parsley
Mornay sauce*	salt and pepper
mushroom duxelles*	butter

Cook the eggs. Following the directions above prepare
   1 hard-boiled egg for each serving.
Prepare the sauce. Make in advance
   Mornay sauce.
Lightly butter a shallow baking dish and spread a thin film of sauce in
the bottom of the dish.
Preheat the oven 375 F (170 C).
Stuff the eggs. Cut each egg in half, lengthwise. Press the yolks through
a fine sieve into a small bowl. For every 4 eggs, blend the yolks with:
   2 Tbs. (30 ml) Mornay sauce,
   1 Tbs. (15 ml) mushroom duxelles,
   1 sprig parsley, minced,
   salt and pepper lightly to taste.
Stuff the egg whites with the yolk mixture and place the eggs over the
sauce in the baking dish. Pour the remaining sauce over the eggs to coat
them lightly. Dot over the top
   1 Tbs. (15 g) butter.
Bake in the preheated oven for 30 minutes.
Variations. Other Sauces for Eggs. To create your own combinations,
consult Chapter 5 for directions for cream, curry, mushroom, paprika, or
Velouté sauce. A pan sauce from braised veal or roasted chicken could
also be used by thickening it with a light roux.† Eggs are sometimes very
simply sauced with browned butter.

METHOD FOR CODDLED EGGS

Cook the eggs. Coddled eggs may substitute for poached eggs in any
recipe and often appear much neater on the serving platter. Use eggs that
are at least three days old; they are easier to peel. If the eggs are colder
than room temperature, set them in a bowl of warm tap water. Fill a heavy
saucepan three-quarters full of hot water and set it on medium-high heat.
When the water has reached a gentle boil, remove the pan from the heat.
Reduce the temperature setting to medium-low. Transfer the eggs to the
saucepan and return the pan to the heat. Stir the eggs to center the yolks.
Simmer for either 5 or 6 minutes depending on how set you prefer the
yolk. Cook the eggs the full 6 minutes, however, if they are to be peeled
and sauced rather than served in egg cups.
Peel the eggs. Transfer the eggs to a bowl filled with cold water.
Continue running cold water into the bowl to stop the eggs' cooking. After

they have set a few seconds, gently tap the ends of each egg to crack its shell and return it to the cold water. Turn off the tap and let the eggs set for at least 10 minutes so that they will compress and shrink from the shell. Gently tap the shell of each egg to crush it completely. Remove the shell by pulling away both the shell and the membrane underneath. Rinse each egg; they are now ready to be sauced.

CODDLED EGGS BORDELAISE ▬▬▬▬▬▬▬▬▬▬▬▬▬▬

Ingredients

coddled eggs (above)	parsley
slices of bread	bay leaf
butter	thyme
shallot or green onion	peppercorns
light Burgundy wine	flour
brown beef stock*	sautéed mushrooms* or
celery	mushroom duxelles*

Traditional recipes for this dish require that eggs be poached in the red wine used in the sauce. However, since the wine unattractively changes the color of the eggs, an alternate method is given here.

Cook the eggs. Using the method described above, coddle and peel

> 1 egg per serving.

Preheat the oven 325 F (150 C).

Toast the canapés. Trim crusts from

> slices of bread, 1 per serving.

Spread the bread lightly with

> butter.

Bake on a rack in the preheated oven for 8 to 10 minutes until they are lightly browned. While they are baking, turn the canapés once to keep them flat.

Prepare the sauce. For 4 eggs, cook together gently in a saucepan until transparent:

> 1 tsp. (5 g) butter,
> 1 shallot or white of 1 large green onion, minced.

Add to the saucepan and boil to reduce to half:

> 1 cup (250 ml) light Burgundy wine,
> 1 cup (250 ml) beef stock,

and a bouquet of herbs:

> 1 celery stalk,
> 3 parsley sprigs,
> ½ domestic bay leaf,
> pinch thyme,
> 2–3 peppercorns.

In a small, heavy skillet cook to a golden brown roux:

> 1 Tbs. (15 g) butter,
> 1 Tbs. (15 g) flour.

Pour the hot, reduced wine stock through a sieve into the roux. Cook and stir until smooth.

Cook the mushrooms. Sauté for each serving

2 medium, sliced mushrooms (or spread the canapés with previously prepared mushroom duxelles).

Assemble the dish. Reheat the eggs briefly in the sauce. Arrange the toasted canapés on individual serving dishes. Spoon the mushrooms over the canapés and place an egg on top. Ladle the sauce over all. Serve immediately garnished with

chopped parsley.

EGGS FLORENTINE ▰▰▰▰▰▰▰▰▰▰▰▰▰▰▰▰▰▰▰▰▰▰▰

Ingredients

braised spinach*
coddled eggs (above)
Mornay sauce*

Prepare the spinach. Cook and arrange in a shallow, buttered casserole

braised spinach.

Cook the eggs. Following the directions given above, coddle and peel

1–2 eggs per serving.

Preheat the oven 350 F (160 C).

Assemble the dish. Place the eggs on the spinach and pour over to cover

Mornay sauce.

Reheat in the preheated oven for 15 to 20 minutes just before serving.

Variations. Garnish, if desired, with one of the following:

chicken livers, sautéed;
sausage or bacon, sautéed;
tongue or ham, cooked and diced;
grilled tomatoes;
asparagus tips, buttered.

METHOD FOR OMELETS

Prepare the eggs. Beat together with a fork only until the yolks and whites are just blended:

2 eggs,
¼ tsp. salt,
2–3 grinds pepper.

Heat the pan. Place in an omelet pan (or cast-iron skillet or lid-skillet as suggested in Chapter 2)

1 Tbs. (15 g) butter.

Set the pan over medium-high heat. Allow the butter to melt and begin to brown lightly. Quickly tilt the pan to coat its bottom and sides with butter.

Add the eggs. Pour the beaten eggs into the skillet all at once.

"Layer" the omelet. Stir the eggs with a fork in a circular motion and at the same time tilt and roll the pan to allow the liquid egg to fill the spaces created by stirring. After a few seconds the eggs will begin to congeal. Be certain that the pan is covered in an unbroken layer of egg.

Add the filling. Spread the filling over the center third of the egg layer in a strip from edge to edge. Let the omelet finish its cooking and browning a few seconds longer, but do not allow the eggs to overcook. Depending on preference, the center should remain slightly liquid or be cooked only until just set. The total cooking time for an omelet is less than half a minute.

Fold the omelet. Run the fork around and under the outside edge of the omelet to loosen any spot that may have stuck to the pan. Lift the handle to tip the pan at a 30° angle to the cooking surface. With the fork, starting from the side closest to the handle, fold ⅓ of the omelet over onto itself. Lift the handle higher tilting the pan at a 60° angle. Make 1 more fold of the omelet. Finally, lifting the pan handle vertically (90° to the cooking surface) turn the omelet out onto a waiting plate. Serve at once.

Suggestions for Omelet Fillings

Fill an omelet with ¼ to ⅓ cup (60-80 ml) of any of the following:

(1) *Ham, bacon, or salt pork.* Dice† and sauté.†

(2) *Croutons.* Dice bread, sauté in butter and season with herbs.

(3) *Potatoes.* Dice and sauté.

(4) *Mushrooms.* Use sautéed* or simmered mushrooms,* or mushroom duxelles.*

(5) *Artichokes.* Use the bottoms or stems, steamed, sliced, and buttered.

(6) *Asparagus.* Use the tender tips, steamed and buttered.

(7) *Cheese.* Select a cheese that can be thinly sliced or grated: Swiss, Edam, Gouda, or Cheddar.

(8) *Tomato sauce.* Also see the note following, Ham in Tomato Sauce.*

(9) *Cream sauce fillings.* Combine diced chicken, ham, shellfish, mushrooms, or other vegetables with cream sauce.*

Desserts

DESSERT CRÊPES

Bake the crêpes. Dessert crêpes may be made from the batter described in Chapter 5. Consult that section for details. Any batter left from making main dish crêpes will keep refrigerated one day and can be used for the next evening's dessert.

Present the crêpes. See the suggestions below.

SERVING SUGGESTIONS

(1) *Jam filling.* Spread crêpes with jam; roll and sprinkle them with confectioner's sugar.

(2) *Au citron.* Dust the underside of the crêpe with granulated sugar; roll and garnish with peeled slices of lemon or orange.

(3) *Custard filling.* Fill crêpes with Custard Crème (below). Roll, or fold in half. Arrange crêpes in a buttered baking dish; sprinkle with granulated sugar and broil a minute or two until glazed.

(4) *Flambéed.* Any of these may be flamed by pouring over a little warmed Cognac and igniting it. †

Wine Guide. See Index, Dessert wines.

CUSTARD CRÈME

Ingredients

    sugar
    flour
    salt
    egg
    milk
    vanilla extract
    whipping cream

This custard is considerably less tricky to put together than the classic crème à l'Anglaise.

Cook the custard. Combine in the top of a double boiler:

    ⅓ cup (80 ml) sugar,
    2 Tbs. (30 g) flour,
    ⅛ tsp. salt.

Beat in

    1 egg.

Pour in, whipping to blend

    ¾ cup (375 ml) scalded milk, cooled slightly.

Cook and stir over boiling water for 5 minutes, then cook an additional 5 minutes, stirring occasionally.

Cool the custard. Remove the pan from the heat and set aside for about 15 minutes.

Final steps. Fold in:

    1 tsp. vanilla extract,
    ½ cup (125 ml) heavy cream, whipped.

Chill the crème in the refrigerator for at least an hour before using.

Tarts and Tartlettes

Prepare the pastry. Well in advance of serving, prepare and bake to completely done

8-inch (20 cm) pastry shell,* or
8 tartlette shells (shaped over an inverted muffin tin).

Fill the pastry. At the last minute before serving, fill pastry shells with
Custard Crème.*

Garnish the tart(s). See below.

Serving Suggestions: Garnishes for Tarts

(1) *Crème chantilly.* Pipe decorative borders around the tart(s) with a mixture of heavy cream beaten very stiff and confectioner's sugar to sweeten.

(2) *Fruit tart(s).* Arrange attractively over the custard drained, canned, or frozen fruits or berries, or poached fresh fruit.

(3) *Nut tart(s).* Sprinkle over toasted nuts, or coconut.

(4) *Glazed tart(s).* Garnish with fresh whole strawberries or sliced bananas and brush with a glaze of melted currant jelly or apricot preserves.

Wine Guide. See Index, Dessert wines.

Fruit Fritters

Directions for making apple and banana fritters* are given on page 125.

Sweet Soufflé

The dessert soufflé follows the same general procedure outlined for main dish soufflés.* Make the following adjustments:

Prepare the pan. Butter the inside and coat it with granulated sugar.

Make the sauce base. Scald
½ cup (125 ml) milk.

At the same time cook the roux† until it is just beginning to turn a golden color:

2 Tbs. (30 g) butter,
1½ Tbs. (25 g) flour.

Add the hot milk all at once to the roux and cook and stir 5 minutes. Remove from the heat and add

1 Tbs. (15 ml) vanilla extract.

Beat together until light:

4 egg yolks,
3 Tbs. (45 g) sugar.

Add the egg yolks and sugar to the base.

Prepare the egg whites. Beat until very stiff, but not dry

5 egg whites.

During the last few moments of beating the whites, sprinkle over
    1 Tbs. (15 ml) sugar.
Final steps. Fold the whites into the base and turn the soufflé into the
prepared pan. Set in the middle level of a preheated 400 F (185 C) oven
and immediately reduce the heat to 375 F (170 C). Bake 18 to 20
minutes.
Serve at once.
Note. The dessert soufflé, once combined, can wait a few minutes
before being baked, but it must be eaten as soon as it is taken from the
oven. Make the base just before starting dinner. Immediately before
baking, beat the egg whites and combine with the base.

Variations. (1) Chocolate. Melt in the scalded milk: 1½ squares un-
sweetened chocolate and 2 Tbs. (30 g) sugar.
    (2) Coffee. Add 2 Tbs. (30 ml) double strength coffee to the base.
    (3) Orange. Omit vanilla and add to the cooked base: grated rind of 1
orange and 2 Tbs. (30 ml) orange juice.
    (4) Lemon. Omit vanilla and add to the cooked base: grated rind of 1
lemon and juice of ½ lemon.
    Wine Guide. See Index, Dessert wines.

DESSERT CHEESE TRAY

This typical weekday French dessert can be readily assembled with
cheeses from American markets. A balanced assortment will include one
cheese from three or four of the types listed below:
    (1) Roquefort or bleu,
    (2) Camembert or Brie,
    (3) Monterey Jack or Wisconsin Müenster,
    (4) Edam or Gouda,
    (5) a sharp cheddar, and
    (6) Swiss: Emmenthal or Gruyére.
Cream cheese may be included on the tray and is also a good sweet
dessert served alone, topped with whipped cream and sprinkled with
sugar and cinnamon. Place bread or crackers (unflavored, such as wheat,
rye, club, or saltine) on the table with a bowl of fruit to accompany the
cheese tray and pour a little more dry table wine from dinner.

Coffeemaking

Dinner is incomplete until it is punctuated at its end with a perfectly
brewed cup of coffee—rich and satisfying. While filter methods make a
dependable, excellent coffee every time, it is also possible to make perfect
coffee in an ordinary six-cup (1.5 l) glass percolator. The pot may be

prepared a little in advance, but it should not be perked until just before it is to be served.

Grind the beans. If you have a blender or coffee grinder, use whole bean coffee, preferably dated for freshness. Grind only the amount needed for a single pot, just before using. For a six-cup (1.5 l) pot measure

⅓ cup (80 ml) coffee beans.

Grind them in the blender on a middle-high speed. Count 12 or 13 seconds and shut off the blender.

Prepare the pot. Fill the pot to the six-cup line with fresh, cold water. Transfer the ground coffee to the basket and fit it onto the stem. Dust from the base of the stem any coffee that filters through before setting the assembled works into the water. If your kitchen is supplied with artificially softened water, do not add the filter ring that covers the basket.

"Perk" the coffee. Set the pot on high heat and watch its progress very carefully: coffee made this way becomes bitter *only if* the water is permitted to boil. When the water has begun to draw up through the stem and is starting to color a little, turn the heat down. With electric heat adjust to a low or medium-low setting. Gas heat should be reduced more gradually in two or three stages. At this point, when the water has begun to color, the coffee is nearly ready. Watch it closely and remove the pot from the heat when it reaches the strength you like, preferably not too strong.

Serve the coffee. Never pour the coffee through the basket of grounds. Remove the works as soon as the coffee has ceased to draw up the stem.

Reheating coffee. Should it be necessary to reheat the coffee, do so *without* boiling. Heat it only until you can see steam wafting up inside the pot and tiny bubbles just beginning to rise from the bottom. Remove immediately from the heat.

Glossary

Definition of Cooking Methods and Terms

Al dente, a term referring to pasta cooking, is a test for doneness. Pasta, when correctly cooked, is tender but firm "to the teeth" when bitten to test. Cooking al dente usually takes 12 to 14 minutes in boiling water over medium-high heat for thin pastas (spaghetti, linguini, macaroni, noodles); lasagna and large shell pastas take longer.

Anglaise coating is a method (of English origin) to prepare foods for deep fat frying. Foods are dipped successively in flour, a mixture of egg and oil, then bread crumbs to form a seal against the hot fat and produce a light, crisp crust (see Index).

Blanching is adding foods to boiling water for a few minutes, usually to remove some undesirable quality such as excessive saltiness (*e.g.* bacon, salt pork) or the slight bitterness of certain vegetables such as turnips, onions, carrots.

Boiling refers to heating liquids and is also a method of cooking. A liquid is brought to a boil over high heat and reaches a full boil when the surface is broken by large air bubbles rising to the top. Cooking in boiling water is the traditional French method for vegetables; meats are never boiled.

Bouquet of herbs provides the basic seasoning for nearly all foods simmered in a liquid. A bouquet is composed of one stalk celery, pinch of thyme, half a bay leaf, and two or three sprigs parsley. Its name comes from the traditional practice of tying the herbs together with string so they will not be skimmed out during initial cooking phases (as in preparing stocks or soups) and for easy removal when the dish is done. The necessity of tying may be circumvented by adding the herbs to the cooking liquid after it has been skimmed.

Braising is a method of meat cookery. Cuts are first browned in a skillet in a mixture of butter and oil (the butter for flavor, the oil to raise the burning point of butter). Browned meats are transferred to a casserole with liquid (water or stock, and wine) to finish cooking in a slow oven. Braising is usually employed with less tender cuts because the slow cooking effectively breaks down fibrous meats. Herein, the term has been applied to procedures of slow cooking vegetables in a rich or savory liquid.

173

Broiling is a method of quickly cooking meats over an open flame or in an open pan under the oven broiler. Beef steaks, lamb chops, poultry, and fish are effectively cooked by broiling, but most require brushing with melted butter to protect surfaces from the heat.

Beurre manié provides a means of thickening liquids to make a sauce. It consists of equal parts of butter and flour, mashed together. Beurre manié is simply stirred into a hot liquid and blended. This technique is used to thicken vegetable cooking liquids.

Closed casserole roasting is a method by which meats are cooked in an oven in a tight-lidded casserole. It is especially recommended for pork and veal (usually browned before adding to the casserole) and for chicken (often roasted in a casserole without initial browning). Unlike the braising method, no liquid is added to the casserole; foods render and cook in their own juices.

Court bouillon is a liquid (water and clam juice, or water only) seasoned with aromatic herbs, used for poaching fish (see, for example, Poached Salmon*).

Deep-frying is a method by which foods are rapidly cooked in several inches of very hot fat. Just before cooking, foods are given a protective covering of batter or Anglaise coating.

Deglazing is a means of releasing the pan residue after browning meats. Remove sautéed meats from the skillet, pour off the sauté fat, and add about ⅓ cup (80 ml) wine and/or stock. Over high heat, scrape the pan to incorporate the brownings. If meats are to braise, add the deglazing liquid to the stock in the casserole. When wine is used it must boil sufficiently to burn off the alcohol. For meats served immediately, continue cooking with deglazing liquid to reduce and thicken to a light sauce, about 2 Tbs. (30 ml). Minced onion or shallot may be added to cook as the liquid reduces. Spread the sauce over the meat.

Dice by cutting foods into small cubes. Cut in slices; cut slices into thin strips (julienne), and then cut the strips into cubes.

Flambéing, for most French dishes, is done in the initial stages of cooking. Heat 2 Tbs. (30 ml) Cognac or brandy for a moment in a small skillet or saucepan. Ignite with care by placing a lighted match near the liquid; it will flame instantaneously. Pour the flaming liquid into the dish in process. To flambé dessert crêpes for serving, follow this procedure also and carry the flaming dish to the table.

Fold by adding ingredients carefully to a mixture so as not to mash or break down. This is done by reaching delicately to the bottom of the container with a spatula or wire whip and lifting out with a circular (folding) motion.

Julienne foods by cutting in narrow, rectangular strips (see Dice).

Mince by dicing or chopping foods very fine.

Parboiling is a means of giving foods an initial partial cooking in boiling water before adding to a dish. It is used to equalize varying cooking times of ingredients.

Parboiling also has the effect of blanching (see above) and the terms are sometimes used interchangeably.

Poaching is a method of slow cooking foods in a gently simmering liquid to cover. It is especially effective with fish and chicken.

Purée is a well-cooked food (usually fruit or vegetable) rendered the consistency of a thick sauce. This is accomplished by mashing, rubbing through a sieve, or processing in a food mill, blender, ricer, or grinder. Purée is also the process of preparing foods in this manner.

Roasting is a dry heat method of cooking meats uncovered in a moderately hot oven. It is used for large, tender cuts such as beef rib roasts, rump or sirloin roasts, and poultry. Roasting sears the meat's exterior, sealing in the juices. After cooking, deglaze the roasting pan with 1 cup (250 ml) liquid (see above).

Roux is a thickening agent for many sauces (see Chapter 5). It consists of equal parts butter and flour, but unlike beurre manié, the mixture is well cooked before liquid is added.

Sautéing is a method of skillet cooking foods in a small amount of good quality fat such as combined butter and oil. See the Index for recipes to sauté chicken, chops, and steaks. Sauté is sometimes used as a general term meaning "to brown" or "to cook in oil."

Simmering is cooking foods in a liquid over low heat so that the surface releases steam but is not broken by air bubbles.

Stew traditionally is a dish in which meat, vegetables, and liquid cook slowly together for several hours until very tender. We have extended the term to include a modern adaptation. Dishes in which vegetables and liquid cook together slowly with cooked meat added a few minutes before serving are also called "stews."

Zest is the outer layer of a citrus fruit containing tiny oil beads.

French Menu Reading Guide

The inclusion of certain phrases in the title of French dishes is a shorthand means of indicating preparation methods, ingredients of a dish, and/or regional characteristics. The following is a guide to what one may expect of some of these traditional terms.

French Regional Cooking Styles
à la Lyonnaise, with lightly browned onions
à la Parisienne, "haute cuisine," usually with cream and mushrooms
à la Provençal, informal with savory herbs, garlic, tomatoes
Alsatian, Germanesque, hearty, often with beer
Bordelaise, usually with red wine and brown sauce
Niçoise, with tomatoes and olives, Mediterranean seasonings (oregano, basil, fennel)
Normande, usually with apples or Calvados (apple brandy of Normandy)

Exotic Cooking Styles

à l'Américaine, usually with tomatoes

à la Flamande, (Flemish) faintly sweet-sour

à la Grecque, with tomatoes, pimento, sometimes sausages

à l'Indienne, with curry powder and sometimes raisins

à l'Orientale, à la Turque, with saffron and tomatoes

Florentine, with spinach

Milanaise, with saffron and/or grated Swiss cheese, butter

Polonaise, with buttered bread crumbs

Cooking Styles, General Terms

à la boulangère, "baker's style," meat roasted on a bed of potatoes

à la maison, specialty "of the house"

à la managère, "housewife's style," informal cookery, meat often browned in
    bacon or pork fat

à la meunière, with browned butter

bonne femme, "good woman," usually simmered in butter, wine, shallots, and
    parsley

chasseur, "hunter style," usually with wine, mushrooms, and tomatoes

marchand de vin, "wine merchant," flavored with wine (reduced)

paysanne, "country style" (*fermière,* "farmer style"), seasoned with onions,
    carrots, diced bacon or salt pork

Dish Ingredients

à la Diable, "Deviled," with mustard

à l'estragon, with tarragon

au beurre, with butter

au fromage, au gratin, with cheese

au Madère, with Madeira wine

aux fines herbs, with parsley, chives, thyme, and chervil

carbonnade, with beer

d'ail, with garlic

printanière, with spring vegetables (carrots, onions, new potatoes, green beans,
    peas)

sauvage, "wild," with game

Preparation Methods

à brun, browned

à blanc, cooked without browning

à l'étuvée, "smothered," cooked slowly in a closely covered pot

à la mode, marinated and braised with the marinade

bouilli, cooked in *court bouillon*†

braisé, braised

chaud-froid, "hot-cold," cooked then chilled as for jellied buffet dishes

composée, composed, arranged

en chemise, en croûte, wrapped in pastry crust, baked

en cocotte, cooked in hot oven in a tightly closed casserole *en daube,* stew of previously marinated meat; marinade forms part of the cooking liquid

en gelée, coated with jellied stock

en papillote, cooked in paper cases

farcie, stuffed

frit, fried

glacé, glazed

grillé, broiled

rôti, roasted

Garnishes for Serving

à la neige, with a "snow" meringue

à la Soubise, with onion purée

amandine, with almonds

persillé, with parsley

Strasbourgeoise, with goose liver and truffles

Veronique, with green grapes

Dishes, General Names

baguette, long loaf of French bread

Bavarois, "Bavarian," mold of custard and whipped cream

beignets, fritters

biscuit à la cuiller, lady finger

blanc mange, milk pudding

blanquette, stew, often of veal, with an egg yolk-thickened white sauce with cream

bouillabaise, soup of assorted Mediterranean fish

brioche, flaky, buttery bread for breakfast or tea

canapé, round of bread toasted or sautéed in butter

cassoulet, bean stew with pork, lamb, and sometimes goose or game

chausson, turnover

civet, stew of furred game

consommé, thin soup of clarified stock

coq au vin, chicken fricasséed in wine

crème, soup made from a thickened, cream-enriched stock base

crème à l'Anglaise, soft custard

croquettes, meat or fish bound by a heavy béchamel sauce,* chilled, shaped, coated, and deep-fried

escabèche, marinated fish

fricadelles, chopped or ground meat patties, sautéed

fricassée, chicken braised in cream, wine, or tomato sauce

gateau, cake, tart, or mold

gelée, gelatin

hachis, hash

mousse, jellied sauce, either a main dish containing meat or fish or a sweet dessert

navarin, lamb stew

pâté, (final e accented) purée of liver with Cognac and seasonings

pâte, pastry
pâte à chou, puff pastry
pâte à Génoise, buttercake
pâte à Savarin, spongecake
paupiettes, meat rolls
potage, thick soup
pot-au-feu, meat and vegetables poached in stock
profiteroles, puff pastry, filled
quenelles, dumplings
quiche, custard pie with meat, cheese, or shellfish for appetizer or main dish
ragoût, stew, usually with vegetables
rissoles, deep-fried pastries
rouelle, casserole
salmis, stew of feathered game
suprêmes, boneless breasts of chicken
turban, ring mold

Index